SHAKESPEARE'S SETTINGS

Shakespeare's Settings

AND A SENSE OF PLACE

Ralph Berry

UNIVERSITY OF WALES PRESS
2016

www.uwp.co.uk

British Library CIP Data
A catalogue record for this book is available from the British Library

ISBN   978-1-78316-808-8
eISBN   978-1-78316-809-5

Designed and typeset by Chris Bell, cbdesign
Printed by CPI Antony Rowe, Chippenham, Wiltshire

CONTENTS

ACKNOWLEDGEMENTS

Chapter One, Chapter Two, Chapter Three, Chapter Four and Chapter Six first appeared in *Contemporary Review*. Chapter Nine is part of an essay, '*Richard III:* Bonding the Audience', from *Mirror up to Shakespeare: Essays in Honour of G. R. Hibbard*, edited by J. C. Gray (University of Toronto Press, 1984, and reprinted with permission of the publisher). Chapter Twelve, 'Ben Jonson at Althorp: Memoir of a Royal Visit' appeared in *Notes and Queries*, and is reprinted with permission of Oxford University Press.

References are to *The Complete Works of Shakespeare*, updated fourth edition, edited by David Bevington (Longman Publishing Group, 1997).

LIST OF
ILLUSTRATIONS

INTRODUCTION

SHAKESPEARE loved settings, locations, the places where human beings live under certain specific conditions. Through the physical milieux we understand the people who dwell in them. I take it to be axiomatic that Shakespeare's intuitive grasp of psychology is the foundation of his drama, and this is reflected in the places where his dramatis personae live.

Man lives in a landscape, always.

This book's prime interest is topography and the special significance of certain settings for Shakespeare's plays, both in performance and in his imaginative re-creation of the milieu. Shakespeare had always a clear idea of his plays' settings, and his dramas show imprints of location-values upon the playwright's mind. I take it for granted that he never left England, but his mind absorbed information from all quarters, and he must have spoken to many travellers from many lands. London, the crossroads of world travel, was ideal for a man of his interests. And he read widely. The great proving ground for all this is *Hamlet*.

It is as certain as anything can be that Shakespeare got his idea of Elsinore – Kronborg Castle, Helsingør – from his three colleagues who had a gig there in the summer of 1586. Will Kemp, George Bryan and Thomas Pope are all recorded in the royal Danish household as having been paid for two months' residence, with a one-month bonus. All three toured on the Continent. Of course they talked about their experiences on tour, as actors do. I suspect that Kemp, a notable self-publicist, talked of little else. When Theseus gracefully declines Bottom's offer of a 'Bergamask dance' at the end of *A Midsummer Night's Dream*, he is putting across a company in-joke. The editorial gloss on 'Bergamask: a rustic dance named after the people of Bergamo in northern Italy' is incomplete without the further information that it is the only recorded citation of the word in the *OED*. Kemp was linked to Bergamo, according to Thomas Nashe. So Theseus is saying to Bottom – played, as we know, by Kemp – in the manner of Mr Bennet, 'You have delighted us long enough.' From this archetypal travel bore Kemp, and from Pope and Bryan, Shakespeare gained first-hand accounts of a royal palace which became the stage set embedded in the text of *Hamlet*. The imaginative fictions took off from the physical realities, and it shows. Kronborg is a massive stage direction, which illuminates the text at many points. The 'platform' (gunsite), 'cannons', 'lobby', 'chapel', 'hall', 'arras' (with 'picture'), all appear in the text and the actuality of Kronborg Castle. Courtyard, terrace and Great Hall are exceptionally suited to the performance of certain phases of *Hamlet*, with the first two being featured in the Hamlets of Richard Burton and Kenneth Branagh. The climate of Helsingør fits in with the short summer night of the opening scene and the coming of the 'dawn in russet mantle clad', when indeed it can be 'a nipping and an eager air'. Shakespeare was well acquainted with the castle and outlook, and may well have studied the illustration of Kronborg in Braun and Hogenberg's *Civitates Orbis Terrarum*. Elsinore is a country of the mind that comes to life in Kronborg Castle, and Kronborg owns the birth certificate of *Hamlet*.

Certain plays are powerfully shaped by Shakespeare's sense of place. Consider the Great Hall of the Middle Temple. It is certain that Shakespeare's company, the Lord Chamberlain's Men, played *Twelfth Night* there on Candlemas, 1602, and it is overwhelmingly likely that Shakespeare – unless he were off sick – took part in that performance. The *Twelfth Night* of that event resembled what we would call Dinner Theatre, laid on for the Serjeants' feast. Even if one does not accept Anthony Arlidge's thesis (*Shakespeare and the Prince of Love*, Giles de la Mare, 2000) that this was the first night, there is a closely argued case that Shakespeare was well familiar with the Middle Temple and its members, and that *Twelfth Night* has clear allusions to the physical features of the Middle Temple Hall. When Kenneth Branagh received the Golden Quill Award of the Shakespeare Guild there in 2000, the guests had a unique opportunity to contemplate a setting which must have featured in Shakespeare's thinking about the text and performance of *Twelfth Night*.

Other locations he knew personally, of the play's setting or at its performance. Haddon Hall in Derbyshire, with its (rare) base court and proximity to the battlements, could well have been the inspiration for the key scene in *Richard II*. It is owned to this day by the Manners family, Dukes of Rutland, and we know that Shakespeare was on good terms with the Earls of Rutland in his day, for he was paid in 1613 for providing an *impresa* to the Earl of Rutland. The Vernon family too had close links with Haddon Hall, and they are favourably treated in the History plays. If future research strengthens the claims of the Lancashire Connection version of Shakespeare's lost years, then Haddon Hall may appear as a map reference point in Shakespeare's travels. Hampton Court Palace was the setting for a command performance of *Hamlet* by the King's Men, put on for St Stephen's Night in 1603. There, King James and Queen Anne (who knew Kronborg well) watched Claudius and Gertrude enact royalty watching a play. The King's Men went on to play regularly at Whitehall for the court. And Shakespeare must have known Windsor, where *The Merry Wives of Windsor* conveys a totally authentic sense of the town. The play could serve as a tourist guide, with a map supplied by Windsor's information bureau. The people of Windsor come to life in Shakespeare's townscape.

There is a wide-ranging general agreement that Shakespeare knew a great deal about Italy, knowledge which he must have picked up from many sources. It is not possible to pin down a particular channel of information, as it is with Kronborg, but Venice is a central presence in two major plays and its location values form the plots. Shakespeare is at pains to establish some kind of familiarity with Venice, if not the Baedeker name-dropping that Jonson went in for in *Volpone*. In *Othello*, 'Lead me to the Sagittar' might well refer to the Frezzeria, the street of the arrow-makers (and today, Harry's Bar). 'What news on the Rialto?' is twice named, in *The Merchant of Venice*, to signal the city's nerve-centre. 'Rialto' and 'gondola' figure in Shakespeare's sense of place. I would argue that everything in *The Merchant of Venice* comes out of a location never named in the play but manifest: the Ghetto. It is the neighbourhood around Shylock's house, including the synagogue, and the home of the Jewish community. One can still visit the Ghetto Vecchio and Ghetto Novissimo, areas enclosed by an urban islet and essentially unchanged. The mind of Shylock becomes more comprehensible as one walks over this small plot of land. As Ian McDiarmid (the RSC Shylock of 1984) found, all the windows in the ghetto looked inward to the square and the synagogue. This formed the basis of the part he played. As Mary McCarthy says, 'The ghetto turned a blind eye to the city.' To walk over Venice is to understand much that is implicit or algebraic in *The Merchant of Venice.*

Other play-settings which Shakespeare cannot have visited but where the location impresses itself on the action, include *The Comedy of Errors*, with its exact sense of Ephesus. Shakespeare knows about the great theatre, and the Harbour Road leading down from it to the sea, and the town's shore culture. He is aware of Rufus of Ephesus, and the advances in psychiatric treatment that were imparted to the Abbess. Beyond the named towns is the sense of space that certain plays impart. Falstaff's tavern gives a uniquely realistic sense of tavern life, and in *Richard III* the many place-names are the underplot of the land bonding in revolt against the tyrant.

In the same vein, I have added a chapter here on Jonson's London, a vista on the same scene that Shakespeare knew. And there is Althorp, the seat of the Spencer family. It was in the grounds of Althorp that Ben Jonson arranged for his Entertainment to be staged, when James I journeyed south from Edinburgh in the summer of 1603. Jonson was commissioned as writer in residence for that great event, and left us a sparkling condensed memoir in his stage directions. The precise spot in the grounds – which were then woodlands – where Queen Anne beheld the Entertainment is not I think discoverable today, but the *genius loci* still governs the site. Here is the birthplace of royal patronage for the Jonsonian masque.

In all this I distinguish between 'place-name' and 'location'. 'Place-name' may be merely a gesture, a garnish. In the text of Shakespeare can be found 'Mexico' and 'Aleppo', which are exotic touches only. There are many such place-names in Shakespeare, some of which extend to the entire play. For example, *Love's Labour's Lost* is set in 'Navarre'. It would be a waste of time to research Renaissance Navarre for clues to the play's provenance. *Love's Labour's Lost* is totally English, and is set in a park owned by the local nobleman (who is also a Justice of the Peace). *Twelfth Night* is set in 'Illyria', but where is that? I have seen an amusing RSC production that was actually set in Illyria, i.e. the Greek coastline, with Sir Toby and Sir Andrew as cost-of-living, cheap-liquor expats. But that was a director's conceit. The main setting for *Twelfth Night* is the substantial Elizabethan house and garden of Olivia. By 'location', and with it a real sense of setting, I understand a place that Shakespeare either knows directly or has imaginative understanding of. In all cases there must be visual impact.

There are some play-settings of which Shakespeare has little visual sense. *The Winter's Tale* can tell us nothing of Sicilia and Bohemia, and a similar lacuna affects the Celtic fringe of the canon. 'Barkloughly Castle call they this at hand?' asks Richard II (3.2.1), a resonant question since he does not even know that the castle, near which he has just landed, is properly known as Harlech. 'Wales' has Milford Haven; what does Milford Haven look like? We have at least a postcard; Shakespeare did not have even that. 'Princely Richmond', we are told, is 'At Pembroke, or at Ha'rfordwest in Wales' (*Richard III*, 5.5.10), and that is all. In the play, Richard II endures his great pivotal scene in 'Flint Castle' (3.3), which Shakespeare cannot have visited in the flesh and is, as I argue, inspired by Haddon Hall. It is hard (though not impossible) to argue that Shakespeare ever crossed the border. His company, on tour, must have played in Ludlow, and that is the nearest that we know of. An outer possibility is that 'Shakeshafte', through the Stanleys, might have a link with Denbighshire and the Salusburys of Llewenni. In 1586 John (later Sir John) Salusbury married Ursula Stanley, the illegitimate daughter of the Earl of Derby, and the couple were regular visitors to her father's estates. The Denbighshire family had close links to the Stanleys and Catholic circles in Lancashire and at court, and

Shakespeare does indeed seem to have got on to an aristocratic network that might have taken him briefly to Wales. To Henslowe, 'Wales' was a cave. (Apparently he had some kind of stage cave to hand.) *Cymbeline*, though set partly in Wales, has no real sense of place, and, if anything, is defined by the deadly insult that Cloten hurls at Guiderius, 'rustic mountaineer'. A 'mountaineer' approximates to the American 'hillbilly', that is, a rustic who dwells above the civilization level of the plains. 'Scotland' is more promising; there is a sense of Dark Age Scotland that defines the values of *Macbeth*, the land being the antithesis to 'peaceful England'. Everything is in the culture. But I do not find that this cultural sense translates into an imaginative and visual apprehension of location. The Scottish names are merely that – Forres, Birnam Wood, Dunsinane, Scone. They are evocative, no more. Of course, Shakespeare never went to Scotland. Nobody did (though the intrepid Jonson made the journey, on foot, in 1618). The high road leading south did not become much beaten until James's accession in 1603, when it started to take on the traffic it does to this day.

Place-name and location: all of them figure in Shakespeare's plays. Locations and settings structure, and sometimes define, the drama. They are a telling dimension of his work. There is more to these locations than I can encompass here: Wilton, for example, where the King's Men put on *A Midsummer Night's Dream*, is surely worth investigation. But I have visited all of the places described in this book. And each of them enhances one's sense of Shakespeare's genius. He comprehended the *genius loci*.

one

SHAKESPEARE'S ELSINORE

'**B**UT what is your affair in Elsinore?' asks Hamlet (1.2.174). Standing in for Horatio, I reply that I am here to visit the town and castle, as guest of the Danish Tourist Board. My objective is to study the location for its bearing on the play. I think that the place tells us a great deal about *Hamlet*.

Kronborg Castle.
© Kronborg Castle/Thomas Rahbek.

Shakespeare conflated the port, Helsingør, and the castle, Kronborg, into one word: Elsinore. The play is clearly set within the castle and its grounds, save perhaps for the graveyard scene (5.1) and 4.4 (the Danish coast). It is Kronborg that matters, a word never mentioned in *Hamlet* but the key to the play. This is the fortress that Frederik II built to enforce Danish command of the Øresund Straits, and with it the power of levying customs duties. The castle/palace was burned down in 1629, then rebuilt by Christian IV with a virtually unchanged exterior. The inner arrangements were modifications rather than radical changes to the original. Hence the Kronborg we see is very close to the Elsinore Shakespeare incorporated into *Hamlet*. The imaginative fictions take off from the physical realities.

The first of these realities to strike one is the sheer military power of the fortress. On two sides of the angle overlooking the Sound are the guns, facing north and east. The gun emplacements are on a terrace, and this is the 'platform' where the action of 1.1 and 1.4–5 takes place ('upon the platform where we watch', says Marcellus, 1.2.213). For the Elizabethans, 'platform' was customarily used to denote a gun site. It is perfectly possible to play those early scenes on the terrace, and this has been done. I even think that Horatio, in 'A mote it is to trouble the mind's eye' (1.1.112) might be punning unconsciously on 'moat', observable from the terrace. The sound of cannon is specified in the text. Claudius makes it a royal ritual to have the cannon salute his drinking, and the last scene has the finest of these effects. 'Let all the battlements their ordnance fire,' says the King (5.2.267). Then comes:

> Give me the cups,
> And let the kettle to the trumpet speak,
> The trumpet to the cannoneer without,
> The cannons to the heavens, the heaven to earth.
> 'Now the King drinks to Hamlet.' (5.2.271–5)

This is a particular stage effect, but Shakespeare never lets us forget that *Hamlet* is rooted in military and political realities, starting with the 'daily cast of brazen cannon' (1.1.76) described in the opening scene. From inside the Great Hall, one looks out through the windows at the gun-terrace

Kronborg Castle courtyard.
© Kronborg Castle/Thomas Rahbek.

just below. And *Hamlet* ends, says Martin Holmes in *The Guns of Elsinore*, 'with the crash of artillery that stood, in so many Elizabethan minds, for the armed might of Denmark' (p. 181).

With military power goes absolute internal security. One feels this as one passes through the outer entrance, which leads under the walls to an open space before the arched entrance to the courtyard. Each side of this space is flanked by a wall with a small window ('The King's Window', dated 1584 and 1585) from which all comers can be scrutinized. They are trapped in a chamber between entrances. These windows realize the sense of surveillance that is everywhere in Kozintsev's film. Through the arch one goes into the great courtyard, which to me is a vivid illustration of the central metaphor, 'Denmark's a prison.' I have never before felt such resonance in the phrase, and in the follow-up references to 'prison' (2.2.241–51). The courtyard, which is almost square, is enclosed on all four sides by the palace elevations. It feels like a prison exercise yard. When Rosencrantz delicately hints at the consequences of Hamlet's mis-behaviour, 'You do surely bar the door upon your own liberty' (3.2.328–9), he is not exaggerating the power behind him. This is a play where doors close, not open. They act as barriers. Nobody gets out of Elsinore if the authorities want to keep them in.

The courtyard is capable of transformation into a theatre. The space would serve admirably for theatrical performances, as it still does. Shakespeare leaves open the setting for the Play Scene in 3.2, so the director can choose to play it indoors (as in the Olivier film) or outdoors (as in the Kozintsev film). It is true that Kronborg courtyard once had a fountain in the centre, subsequently removed by the Swedes. But this fountain could have been turned off for theatrical performances, and its platform remains. Currently it is raised about 5 inches above ground and could easily be built up with temporary structures into a proper stage.

The chambers within Kronborg are directly reflected in the play. The 'chapel' to which the body of Polonius is removed (4.1.37) remains on view. 'The Queen's Closet', as Shakespeare terms it, must be included in what are now called 'the Queen's Rooms'. They are connected by a short corridor with 'the King's Rooms'. 'Lobby' calls for commentary. When Polonius speaks of Hamlet walking 'Here in the lobby' (2.2.161), he does not have in mind our sense of 'entrance-hall', as in a hotel. 'Lobby' means 'a passage or corridor connected with one or more apartments in a building, or attached to a large hall, theatre, or the like; often used as a waiting-place or ante-room' (*OED*, sense 2). Ben Jonson added the word 'gallery'. This is the sense that Hamlet conveys with 'you shall nose him as you go up the stairs into the lobby' (4.3.36–7), when a gallery on an upper floor is indicated.

The most striking interior feature is the Banqueting Hall, or Great Hall. This is vast, one of the largest interiors in Europe. And it contains (as it did in Shakespeare's time) many tapestries portraying Danish roy-alty, for which Kronborg was famous. Polonius, in hiding behind the 'arras'– the word is thrice mentioned – is taking advantage of the space between the hanging screen of tapestry and the wall. *Hiding behind* is the main associate of 'arras', but there is a front too, and Shakespeare makes use of it in the Closet Scene: 'Look here upon this picture, and on this; / The counterfeit presentment of two brothers' (3.4.53–4). The mainstream interpretation of 'picture' is 'miniature painting', and it would be decorous of Hamlet to carry a miniature of his dead father. But there is no reason why the two pictures should be of the same genre. The stage has sometimes used medallions, and even coins, to convey images of the late King Hamlet. Above all, the Kronborg tapestries are portraits of past and present kings; and one or more of them might perfectly well be on the wall of Gertrude's closet.

Harold Jenkins, in his Arden *Hamlet*, is dismissive of the hint:

> The idea that Shakespeare had in mind the portraits of the Danish kings in a famous tapestry in the castle of Kronborg at Elsinore (Jan Stefansson, *Contemporary Review*, LXIX, 25–9, and others) is no more than a pleasant fancy. Theories of life-size portraits in the form of wall paintings or tapestries hanging on the stage, though often confidently asserted, are without substance. *Der Bestrafte Bruder-mord*, in which Hamlet says 'Dort in jener Gallerie hangt das Conterfait Eures ersten Ehegemahls, und da hangt das Conterfait des itzigen', and the famous illustration in Rowe's Shakespeare (1709), with its portraits hanging over the Queen's head, afford some evidence, however we interpret it, of stage practice in a later period, but none at all for Shakespeare's. (p. 518)

This is extraordinary certitude. How can Jenkins know when a stage tradition originated? *Der Bestrafte Brudermord* is a degenerate descendant of the *Hamlet* play that was part of the repertory performed by the English actor John Green and his touring company in Dresden in 1626. That is close enough to Shakespeare's day. Shakespeare intended a strategic ambiguity. He knew about the Kronborg tapestries, many of which are still in place. His lines give the actors maximum flexibility. If a tapestry with a portrait-design or wall-painting is available for a production, well; if not, a small stage property such as a miniature is serviceable, convincing and easy.

If Denmark is a prison, the escape route is the sea. The sea is the great symbol of Hamlet's liberation, taking on dramatic intensity in certain scenes. Kronborg is only a few yards away from the sea, but Shakespeare introduces some dramatic exaggeration here. The flat shore of the Straits is not like the rock-girt coast that Horatio evokes in

> What if it tempt you toward the flood, my lord,
> Or to the dreadful summit of the cliff
> That beetles o'er his base into the sea ... (1.4.69–71)

There is however a remarkable congruence between the sea vista, from Kronborg, and the intimations of the play. It is tellingly expounded by Hugh Hunt. In June 1950 he took his Old Vic production of *Hamlet* (with Michael Redgrave) to Kronborg. They arrived from Zürich in late afternoon, and after supper at their hotel, the Marienlyst, they went on to the castle for the first rehearsal:

All went smoothly until after midnight, when, the castle 'bell then beating one', we were surprised by the loud singing of a blackbird which in the strange stillness of those grey walls was peculiarly distracting. Smoking is strictly forbidden in the castle courtyard and we broke off to enjoy a cigarette on the grass rampart overlooking the sea. Our surprise was considerable when on emerging from the moonlit courtyard we saw the dawn breaking over the Swedish coast opposite us. It was a russet dawn; the sea was the colour of dried blood, and, stranger than all, the comparatively flat Swedish coastline assumed, by virtue of the rising sun, the appearance of 'yon high eastward hill'. Just then a cock crowed, and we knew how it was that Horatio and the watch observed the dawn so shortly after midnight – 'the dawn with russet mantle clad' that frightened the ghost from the battlements.[1]

That looks like serious evidence of Shakespeare's local knowledge. He knew that at high summer the dawn comes not so long after midnight, at this latitude. Of course, ''Tis bitter cold' (1.1.8) points the other way, as does 'The air bites shrewdly, it is very cold' (1.4.1). But these hints are not decisive for a winter setting. Knight stressed that in northern Europe 'The air bites shrewdly' during the interval between sunset and sunrise, even in early summer. He added that Ophelia's flowers – pansies, columbines, and daisies – belong not to winter but to late spring. Besides, what was King Hamlet doing, 'sleeping in my orchard' (1.5.59) two months earlier? It is perfectly Shakespearean to conflate phenomena that are logically incompatible. The opening scene moves from midnight to dawn; and the audience can take this as dramatically compressed time, or a literal rendering in which stage time equals real time.

As Hunt viewed it, the low Swedish coastline took on the appearance of 'yon high eastward hill' (1.1.167). That line has been interpreted differently. Martin Holmes says that Shakespeare made 'a famous error' here. The illustration of Kronborg in a contemporary Elizabethan work, the *Civitates Orbis Terrarum* of Braun and Hogenberg, depicts a high hill facing Kronborg. So Shakespeare might have used that cue for a touch of dramatic exaggeration. At all events, Shakespeare depicts a view from the battlements that faces east, over the Sound. And so it does.

What emerges from seeing Kronborg is Shakespeare's familiarity with castle and outlook. *Hamlet* is well grounded in topography, both architecture and setting. To adopt the untranslatable French term for the uniqueness of a vineyard, Shakespeare knows his *terroir*. But how could he have acquired this knowledge? The answer is beguilingly simple, and irrefutable. Three of Shakespeare's colleagues had been on the Danish payroll.

English players are known to have travelled on the Continent in the late sixteenth century. In 1585, 'certain unnamed English played (*lechte*) in the courtyard of the town hall at Elsinore, when the press of folk was such that the wall broke down'.[2] Next season, the English followed up their success. We have it from the Household Accounts of the Danish court, which for August and September 1586 record:

> 36 daler paid to William Kemp, instrumentalist, for two months' board for himself and a boy, by name Daniel Jonns, which sum he had earned from 17 June when he was engaged, there till one month granted on his dismissal, in all three months, each month 12 daler.

The accounts also mention five other *instrumentister och springere* who were at court from 17 June to 18 September 1586. As the words indicate, they were all-round entertainers, skilled musicians and tumblers. Two of the five names stand out. One was 'Jurgenn Brienn', who has to be George Bryan. The other is 'Thomas Pape', who in his next engagement in Dresden becomes 'Tomas Papst'. He is easily recognizable as Thomas Pope. The three players with experience of the Danish court come into Shakespearean focus with the publication of the Folio in 1623. Immediately before the first play (*The Tempest*) is printed 'The Names of the Principall Actors in all these Plays'. The twenty-six names as printed include William Kempt, Thomas Poope and George Bryan. I do not know if it has been noted before that these three names are given in sequence (numbers 5–6–7 on the list) as if they comprised a natural grouping. One would expect these travelled players to talk about their experiences on the Continent. Their account of Denmark would have entered Company folklore.

Whether Shakespeare had more intimate conversations with the three is impossible to guess. Kemp was much the most famous. He pulled off a notable stunt in 1600, dancing all the way from London to Norwich. Today, this feat would be a charity run; then, it was simple self-publicizing. Kemp played many important clown roles, including Bottom and Dogberry, but he left Shakespeare's company, the Chamberlain's Men, in 1599. We do not know if he played Falstaff: David Wiles (*Shakespeare's Clown*) is sure he did, William Empson had doubts. Kemp was unquestionably a leading member of the company. I think Shakespeare must have had at least a good working relationship with him before the parting of the ways.

The other two are shadowy figures, for whom biographical sketches can be found in the second volume of Chambers, *The Elizabethan Stage*. Pope is referred to in the 1593 list of Strange's Men as 'Mr Pope'. The 'Mr' is significant; it means that he was on a higher footing than the rest, and had a share in the company and its profits. It is Gentlemen and Players in embryo, with the upper echelon being styled differently from the run-of-the-mill players. (Those who recall the English cricket team lists, up to the early 1960s, will recognize a characteristic English practice.) A contemporary satire mentions Pope:

> What means Singer then,
> And Pope the clown, to speak so boorish, when
> They counterfaite the clownes upon the Stage?
>   (Samuel Rowlands, 1600)

from which he appears as one of those Clowns whom Hamlet so disliked: 'And let those that play your clowns speak no more than is set down for them' (3.2.38–9). Playwrights have seldom enjoyed warm relationships with actors who embroider the sacred texts. I cannot see Pope and Shakespeare as soulmates. Bryan looks more promising. He too sported the 'Mr' (like Shakespeare, of course) in an early list. Probably he left the Chamberlain's Men to become an ordinary Groom of the Chamber. He held this post at Elizabeth's funeral in 1603, and still held it in 1611–13. Bryan looks to me more socially attuned and adept than the two clown specialists. He would be a better guide to the customs of Danish royalty, and might well have played on his expertise to become Groom of the Chamber.

The professional connections between Shakespeare and his three colleagues are certain. Shakespeare must have encountered Will Kemp, Thomas Pope and George Bryan on innumerable occasions. Whether he had intimate conversations with one or more, or drew on company folklore for its account of Kronborg, cannot be established and is not important. What matters is that Shakespeare knew his Kronborg. 'Elsinore', as we pass through it today, is a country of the mind that comes to life, a site that glows with Shakespearean illumination. To see it is to come closer to understanding *Hamlet*. As the jockeys know, you have to walk over the course.

Notes

1. Hugh Hunt, *Old Vic Prefaces* (Routlege & Kegan Paul, 1954), p. 51.
2. E. K. Chambers, *The Elizabethan Stage*, 4 vols, II (Clarendon Press, 1923), p. 272.

two

ELSINORE REVISITED

SCENE: the courtyard of Kronborg Castle. 'The air bites shrewdly, it is very cold,' says Hamlet. Horatio agrees: 'It is a nipping and an eager air.' The Danes, knowing their climate, have brought blankets to huddle in and hire more at the interval. But it is still a notable occasion. The Birmingham Repertory Theatre has brought its *Hamlet* (2001)

Kronborg Castle in winter.
© Kronborg Castle/Thomas Rahbek.

to Kronborg Castle, Helsingør – Shakespeare's Elsinore. And Kronborg owns the birth certificate of *Hamlet*.

For the English players have been here before. In 1585 they toured in Helsingør and were a sensation. The citizens tore down a hoarding for a better view. The English players followed up this success, and next season fixed up a gig at the royal palace (which was then located in Helsingør, not Copenhagen). Their names are still there on the Danish payroll, three of them Shakespeare's colleagues – Will Kemp, Thomas Pope, George Bryan. When they came back to England they talked about their touring experiences, as actors do. Shakespeare listened. He gained a set of first-hand accounts of a castle, which became stage directions embedded in the text of *Hamlet*.

Hence *Hamlet* productions at Kronborg have a unique vibrancy. Modern memory goes back to Olivier, who in 1937 was due to star in Tyrone Guthrie's production in the castle courtyard with the Old Vic company. He was then in the throes of an intense affair with Vivien Leigh, who had insisted on joining the company at Helsingør to play Ophelia. 'We could not keep from touching each other,' wrote Olivier.[1] Rehearsals went well, but the summer weather was atrocious. At 7.30 on the first night, 'the rain was coming down in bellropes'.[2] Cancellation was impossible: it was a royal command performance, and the special train bearing the notables had already left Copenhagen. So Guthrie and Lilian Baylis decided to put on *Hamlet* in the ballroom of the Marienlyst Hotel.

The logistics were staggering. Buses carried the company to Kronborg Castle – over a mile from the hotel – where they gathered up costumes, props, make-up. All had to be packed up and transported to bedrooms at the hotel, in an hour and a half. Guthrie made a chalk circle in the centre of the ballroom to mark the playing area, and the press helped to arrange 870 basket chairs. As Alec Guinness remembered it (in *Blessings in Disguise*), the pocket-size stage had room for an upright piano, a pot-ted palm, and a three-piece band. Guthrie delegated all staging decisions to Olivier, who took command with great verve. Guthrie's instructions to the players were terse:

> Suggest you use the platform for Claudius and Gertrude in the play
> scene. Get rid of the piano. I love the palm ... Use any entrance you

can find. Polonius, use the service door. When you are killed wrap yourself in those vulgar velvet curtains. Rather startling. Be polite to Kings and Queens if they get in your way.[3]

Guinness had the most effective entrance in these extraordinary circumstances. 'Alec, make your entrance as Osric through the French windows.' 'But, Tony, they give on to the beach. There's a roaring wind, heavy seas and lashing rain.' 'Arrive wet. Very dramatic.' And it was so. Guinness had to wait his cue on the beach, soaked to the skin. His Danish dresser handed him a large schnapps. 'Skol! Then another schnapps. Skol! Tusen tak. Tak for tusen. Tit for tat. When I blew in through the French windows (which I shut very carefully) I was decidedly unsteady, more like a weary Greek messenger than a Tudor fop.'[4]

Yet it all went superbly. The cast achieved miracles of improvisation, and the audience was totally caught up in 'the most exciting theatrical experience most of us had ever had', as Guinness remembered it. 'Royalty looked pleased, ambassadors clapped their white-gloved hands,' as Guthrie reported in his memoir. Then royalty 'climbed back into their limousines and retreated to the safety of Copenhagen, leaving the Marienlyst Hotel to our excited, undoubtedly drunken mercy. Many bedroom doors were locked, or slammed, or opened that night.'[5] One thing marred the performance. The best entrance to the hotel ballroom, a double door at the head of a short flight of steps, was strictly forbidden. Why? Next morning the head porter showed Guthrie. In the architrave by the doorway was a nest of a pair of blue-tits. The little hen, nervous but gallant, fluttered above our heads. 'If this door had been used, she would have deserted her eggs; you wouldn't have liked that.'[6]

Next year it was a German *Hamlet* at Kronborg, with Hermann Goering the special guest. Gielgud came in 1939, a much-admired performance; Gielgud was then the 'definitive' Hamlet. He was thought, however, to be 'more parlour than platform', and it is true that the robust playing conditions of the Kronborg courtyard do call for a muscular and projective playing style. After the war the Old Vic returned, with Michael Redgrave in the title role in 1950.[7] This was a dignified and intellectual Hamlet, perhaps missing something of the emotional range the part calls for. I would place him as opposite in style to Richard Burton, who

came with the Old Vic in 1954. Burton had above all presence and cha-
risma. (During a run of *King John* with the same Old Vic company, the
director had to scrap his idea of keeping Burton on stage at all times, as
Fauconbridge/Chorus. Nobody could take their eyes off Burton. Silent
and unmoving, he destroyed the production.) The Danish critics saw
Burton's Hamlet as lacking the nobility and subtlety of his predecessors.
But Claire Bloom's Ophelia was striking, and, says Melvyn Bragg without elaboration, 'There were high jinks and mad nights.'[8]

In 1964, the BBC filmed a TV production, *Hamlet at Elsinore*,
in conjunction with Danmarks Radio. Philip Saville directed
Christopher Plummer in the lead role. Michael Caine played Horatio,
his only Shakespearean part, and recalled some of the difficulties of
location shooting:

> The castle had just been redecorated, so although it was the genuine
> article it looked artificial, and they had to dirty it down. But the big-
> gest problem was the fog, not because of the light but because of the
> fog-horn. The castle is on the shore of the straits that pass between
> Denmark and Sweden, and the fog-*horn* was on the castle roof;
> and sounded every fifteen minutes. Poor Christopher Plummer.
> We would all stand ready to shoot and wait for the fog-horn to
> go, Philip would shout, 'Action!' and Christopher would try to get
> through a long soliloquy before the next blast. Not an ideal way to
> do Shakespeare but it added speed and energy and not a little sus-
> pense to some of our performances.[9]

There followed a fifteen-year gap with English Hamlets. Derek
Jacobi's performance with the Old Vic (1979) must have resembled his
BBC-TV Hamlet, of which Clive James wrote that 'Elsinore was set in
a velodrome … you kept expecting cyclists to streak past on the banking
while the Prince was in mid-soliloquy'.[10] But Jacobi's was a cultivated,
Renaissance prince out of Castiglione's *The Courtier* (1528). After the
somewhat eccentric Hamlet of David Threlfall (1986), Kenneth Branagh
came to Kronborg with his Renaissance Theatre Company in 1988. This
was his youthful marker for the full-text film of *Hamlet* that he made
in 1996. Branagh must have been ideally cast for a courtyard Hamlet.

His style is physical, flamboyant, not at all reluctant to court comparison with Fortinbras. Indeed, his film makes Hamlet's last soliloquy, 'How all occasions do inform against me,' ending in 'O, from this time forth, my thoughts be bloody, or be nothing worth' into a pre-intermission aria. With a stirring martial soundtrack, it is set against the snow-clad background of Blenheim Castle.

And this brings us to the recent *Hamlet*s I have seen in Kronborg, from both of which Fortinbras was missing. In 2000 the Royal National Theatre brought John Caird's production to Kronborg. Simon Russell Beale's Hamlet was much admired in England: highly intellectual, a great analyser of his soliloquies. But he was also, and this matters in the courtyard, not a physically compelling Hamlet. Of his performance in London, the *Daily Telegraph* reviewer wrote with suave accuracy that 'He speaks "O that this too too solid flesh would melt" with rare authority'. I must say that Gertrude's 'He's fat and scant of breath' did seem to be levelled at her son, and not, as some scholars suggest, at Laertes. When Russell Beale's Hamlet defeated the trim, athletic Laertes I wanted to call out 'Fixed!' There was no Fortinbras to suggest invidious comparisons with Hamlet; and the text ended on 'And flights of angels sing thee to thy rest'. That was the way they did it throughout the Victorian era. But the Kronborg setting always makes up for whatever limitations may be perceived in Hamlet. One of the National Theatre retainers said to me, 'Personally, I loved the way the live sounds of gulls and chiming clocks blended with the performance.'

The pace of *Hamlet*s then quickened. *Hamlet Sommer 2001* saw the Birmingham Repertory Theatre bring Bill Alexander's production to Kronborg. Richard McCabe, charismatic and fervently energetic, was born for an open-stage Hamlet. His 'antic disposition' was unnervingly real. 'An actor', said Michael Goldman, 'is a man who wants to play Hamlet.' McCabe must have wanted it badly, for he played four acts in bare feet. My heart went out to a man whose feet had to pound the cold stones of Kronborg during the many, fast-running entrances and exits. It was, as he said elatedly to me at the reception afterwards, 'freezing'. McCabe looked like a man who could handle his rapier (by no means true of all Hamlets; in spite of what they say, they have *not* been 'in continual practice'). He had however no Fortinbras to measure himself against, which I thought a pity. A true hero needs a rival. The Dane needs his Norwegian role model. Otherwise Hamlet's universe is ruled by introspection (as in Peter Brook's chamber *Hamlet*, also lacking a Fortinbras). So Alexander's production ended shortly after 'And flights of angels sing thee to thy rest', with a few of Fortinbras's clean-up operation lines being re-assigned to Horatio. 'L'intendance suivra,' as the French military say. Nowadays one might as well wait for Godot as for Fortinbras.

Of the two great scenarios contained in *Hamlet*, the 'political' and the 'private' or 'domestic' dimension, the private/domestic is now much the dominant and fashionable. One sees Gertrude and Claudius as a middle-aged couple *en secondes noces*, trying to make a go of their new marriage and getting no help at all from the son inherited from her previous marriage. Hamlet from this view is a misfit and gifted troublemaker, whose psychic objective is to destroy his mother's second marriage. No wonder Claudius moves from 'Our son' to 'your son'.

However, what Kronborg calls for is a 'political' *Hamlet*. The great palace/fortress is itself a political fact of the first order. It radiates upon the play its own stage directions. The highlighted words in the text become living realities close to the actors' space. The courtyard is a 'prison', with total security of access and exit. Off it is the 'chapel', where the body of Polonius is laid to rest. Upstairs is the 'lobby' where Hamlet walks (as in the galleries of the great English country houses, the noble residents take exercise there). Gertrude and Hamlet meet in 'the Queen's Rooms'. Polonius hides behind the 'arras', one of the famous tapestry-paintings that still adorn the palace walls. The fencing match takes place in the Great Hall ('here in the hall'). The play is made for the castle.

Helsingør may yet come to rival Bayreuth and Salzburg. *Hamlet* may be international and intercultural, as Peter Brook's production at the Bouffes-du-Nord shows. But its true setting is the Baltic power centre of Shakespeare's day. We tend to think of Helsingør as made famous by *Hamlet*, but in Shakespeare's day it was the other way round. He paid homage to a great map-reference point of northern Europe, a focus of military and political power.

Kronborg is a unique and authentic presence. The watchtower/lighthouse is what particularly commended the setting to Jan Kott, at a performance which began at dusk:

in its second half, the beam from a lighthouse placed in a tower of Elsinore castle swept the scaffolding erected in the courtyard with its light, yellow and red in turn. Hamlet's father's ghost appeared on real battlements, and his voice reached the audience from there.[11]

The spotlights on the walls of the old castle make the surroundings interact with the play, making it a *son et lumière* show. Here, one feels, the great play has come home. As the Danes like to say, 'Kronborg to the starboard.'

Notes

1. Laurence Olivier, *Confessions of an Actor* (Weidenfeld and Nicolson, 1982), p. 78.
2. Tyrone Guthrie, *A Life in the Theatre* (Hamish Hamilton, 1961), p. 170.
3. Alec Guinness, *Blessings in Disguise* (Hamish Hamilton, 1985), p. 75.
4. Guinness, *Blessings in Disguise*, p. 75.
5. Guinness, *Blessings in Disguise*, p. 76.
6. Guthrie, *A Life in the Theatre*, p. 171.
7. 'In the huge courtyard of Kronborg Castle, with the accompaniment of sirens in the Sound and riveting in the neighbouring shipyard, the English actors re-shaped their performances in the open air' (Richard Findlater, *Michael Redgrave, Actor* (William Heinemann, 1956), p. 94). Kronborg does lend itself to off-stage effects, and the riveting would suit the arms-race passage of 1.1.
8. Melvyn Bragg, *Richard Burton: A Life* (Little, Brown, 1988), p. 97.
9. Michael Caine, *What's It All About?* (Century, 1992), p. 161.
10. Clive James, *Glued to the Box* (Picador, 1983), p. 93.
11. Jan Kott, *Theatre Notebook 1947–1967* (Methuen, 1968), pp. 208–10.

three

SHAKESPEARE AT THE MIDDLE TEMPLE

Twelfth Night As Dinner Theatre Revisited

When the Shakespeare Guild made its annual Golden Quill award to Kenneth Branagh in January 2000, they chose well in staging the award ceremony at the Middle Temple. There are genuine Shakespearean associations, and the Great Hall held some five hundred celebrants. 'All that was most sonorous of name and title', as Evelyn

Middle Temple Gardens.
Courtesy of the Honourable Society of the Middle Temple.

Waugh wrote (in *Decline and Fall*) of another occasion, 'was there for the beano.' Place is authenticity, the experience we all yearn for. The Great Hall of the Middle Temple – not open to the general public – is a secular temple to Shakespeare. Shakespeare knew it and almost certainly acted there. There's more outside, for Shakespeare makes the pivotal scene in Part One of *Henry VI* take place in the Temple Garden. He imagines the quarrel of the roses to have started among a group of high-spirited aristocrats: 'Within the Temple Hall we were too loud; / The garden here is more convenient' (2.4.3–4). Surely Shakespeare must have walked in the Temple Garden. But the grand association is with *Twelfth Night*.

'I delight in masques and revels sometimes altogether,' says Sir Andrew Aguecheek (*Twelfth Night*, 1.3.108). It's his wistful tribute to the good life. *Revels* was an intense word for the Elizabethans. It resonated. The grind of daily life regularly exploded into festive mirth, whether determined by the calendar or a special event such as a wedding. The spirit of revelry haunts *Twelfth Night*; it's the inspiration for the sub-plot, the gulling of Malvolio. But which revels does the comedy aim at?

The question comes up with Shakespeare's 'occasional' plays. *The Merry Wives of Windsor* was very probably written for the Garter installation of 1597. *A Midsummer Night's Dream* seems to have been written with a noble wedding in mind. Philostrate is the Athenian equivalent of the Master of the Revels, and is ordered by Duke Theseus to 'Stir up the Athenian youth to merriment; / Awake the pert and nimble spirit of mirth' (1.1.12). Theseus promises to wed Hippolyta 'with pomp, with triumph, and with revelling' (1.1.19). We can't be sure of the occasion the play was written to grace; it might have been the wedding of Elizabeth Vere and the Earl of Derby (1595) or Elizabeth Carey and Thomas Berkeley (1596). And the same doubt occurs with *Twelfth Night*.

At first this doubt may seem displaced. Surely Shakespeare must have written *Twelfth Night* for a premiere on Twelfth Night, 6 January? That was the argument of Leslie Hotson, who reckoned, in *The First Night of 'Twelfth Night'*,[1] that the play was part of a gala entertainment at court on 6 January 1601. He resurrected some remarkable diplomatic documents, including the eyewitness report of the Russian ambassador, Grigori Mikulin, to his master, Tsar Boris Fedorovich. The book is a researcher's tour de force. But none of the distinguished guests stopped to report such trifling details as the name of the play and its author. Hotson could not nail down the identification.

Subsequent editors have been uniformly sceptical. This is true of the Arden Shakespeare edition of *Twelfth Night*, edited by J. M. Lothian and T. W. Craik (1975), the New Cambridge edition of Elizabeth Story Donno (1985) and the Oxford Shakespeare edition, edited by Roger Warren and Stanley Wells (1994). There are intricate and powerful reasons for doubting Hotson's claim. It does seem odd that Don Virginio Orsino, Duke of Bracciano, in his reference to the 'commedia mescolata, con musiche e balli' which he saw, never mentions his own name as being one of the dramatis personae. And that was in a letter to his wife Flavia. The editors are surely right that Shakespeare took the name 'Orsino' in the aftermath of the Duke's arrival in London, not as a way of celebrating his presence.

So Shakespeare wrote *Twelfth Night*, in all probability, in the latter part of 1601. A decisive theory on its provenance comes from *Shakespeare and the Prince of Love: The Feast of Misrule in the Middle Temple*.[2] Its author, Anthony Arlidge, is a Queen's Counsel at the Middle Temple, where he is Master of the Entertainments. He is deeply versed in the archives and traditions of the Middle Temple. He puts forward a beguiling and persuasive thesis, that *Twelfth Night* had its premiere in Middle Temple Hall on 2 February 1602.

Of a performance there we have sure knowledge. It is our first sighting of the play. John Manningham was a fourth-year student at the Middle Temple, one of the four Inns of Court. For 2 February 1601 he made this entry in his diary: 'at our feast wee had a play called Twelve Night or What You Will … a good practise in it to make the Steward beleeve his Lady widdowe was in Love with him by counterfeyting a letter as from his lady in generall tearmes …' This has to be Shakespeare's comedy. Could it have been a first night performance?

It could indeed, and Mr Arlidge builds up a very strong case based on circumstantial evidence. As we are sometimes reminded in media reports of court cases today, 'circumstantial' is not an inferior form of evidence. Often it is the only form of evidence available. The date, 2 February, was known to the Elizabethans as Candlemas. The feast of Candlemas was, says Anthony Arlidge, 'one of the two most important dates in the Inn calendar, when members of the Inn who had gained professional preferment were sumptuously entertained'.[3] There's a strong thematic connection: Twelfth Night marked the end of the Christian festival, and exploited the medieval tradition of misrule. The records of student revels at the Inn showed them electing a Prince of Misrule (in the Middle Temple, the Prince of Love) whose reign ended on 2 February. So the theme of misrule in *Twelfth Night* ('this uncivil rule', says Malvolio, 2.3.123) was apt for the Candlemas performance. A comedy of love would have suited a performance in the Kingdom of Love, ruled over by the Prince D'Amour.

The play would have suited the commissioning authorities too. John Shurley was Treasurer of the Middle Temple in 1602, and hoped to be made Serjeant (a well-rewarded honour). A splendid entertainment laid on by the Treasurer would impress the existing Serjeants. (The strategy worked for Sir Robert Spencer at Althorp, in 1603: see Chapter Twelve.) Shakespeare, of course, was by then known as the finest playwright in the land. A new comedy of his, put on by the Chamberlain's Men, would not have come cheap. Mr Arlidge links the name of Shurley to the 'Sophy' (Shah) references in the play, for Robert and Anthony Sherley, family connections of Shurley, travelled to Persia in 1599. Robert Sherley, 'fencer to the Sophy', was painted by Van Dyck in 1622, as was also his wife, a Circassian Christian noblewoman and a renowned beauty, Teresia Khan.[4] Thus the 'Sophy' references are a compliment to the Treasurer and his renowned kin. It all fits together nicely.

So does the topography of the hall. Feste has a striking description of the house in which Malvolio is imprisoned: 'Why, it hath bay windows transparent as barricadoes, and the clerestories towards the south-north are as lustrous as ebony' (4.2.35–6). Shakespeare is clearly making an in-joke – 'Inn-joke' is irresistible – for his special audience. Arlidge puts it definitively: 'The building is clearly not a theatre and the description matches Middle Temple Hall, which has clerestories in the south and north walls, and bay-windows, and is exceptionally light for a building of this kind.'[5] No doubt the staging kept Malvolio in some kind of shadow, easily arranged, so that he could not see what everyone else could. 'The joke is about a light building, and the Hall was one of the first to use new glass technology to produce a large light room.'[6]

Stained glass windows in Middle Temple Hall.
Courtesy of the Honourable Society of the Middle Temple.

These and other allusions read as integral to the text, not as bits stuck on to a pre-existent text. It does look as though Shakespeare had a particular audience in mind. Which would make *Twelfth Night* a custom-written, new play. There's a piece of contributory evidence here. Manningham started to write 'Mid', then crossed it out and wrote 'Twelve Night'. Either way he got it wrong. Was he unsure of the title of the play he had just seen? That too points towards a new play, whose title did not come automatically to the mind of the diarist.

Other allusions sound like contemporary spice, introduced to tickle legal palates. Sir William Knollys, Comptroller of Her Majesty's Household, has long been suspected to be the origin of Malvolio. They

match at several points. He too was a 'Steward', and Malvolio's statement that he will quench his familiar smile 'with an austere regard of
control (2.5.55) sounds like a pun on Knollys's office. There are 'yellow
stockings' allusions in a contemporary ballad mocking Knollys, who
notoriously had made a fool of himself by his infatuation with Mary
Fitton, a young lady at Court under his protection. He wanted to marry
her, once his (much older) wife had died. But his wife remained obsti-
nately alive, and Mary Fitton got pregnant by the Earl of Pembroke
(who refused to marry her). The episode did nothing for Knollys's reputation. Knollys = Malvolio is a set of outrageous hints, which would
have been devoured by a sharp-witted audience. This is not a case, I
suspect, where one leans on Fanny Trollope's great line in these matters:
'Of course, I draw from life, but I always pulp my acquaintances before
serving them up. You never recognize a pig in a sausage.'

We are swimming through a shoal of allusions that would make
sense to the lawyers. 'Curio' and 'Fabian', minor characters in the play,
are nicknames which often occur in student satires and epigrams in the
Middle Temple. That is, they were real people who would have been
present at the performance. 'The lady of the Strachy married the yeoman of the wardrobe' turns out to be a clear hit at one William Strachey
of Gray's Inn, who really had a business connection with the Yeoman
of the Wardrobe (and whose private habits might have been satirized in
'Lady'). Heartless laughter from the audience at this point, as I guess.
Shakespeare bonded with that audience.

In the same vein, Anthony Arlidge makes the attractive suggestion
that *Troilus and Cressida* (1603), a play often suspected of having been
written for an Inns of Court audience, makes an early strike for complicity. The Prologue says:

> our play
> Leaps o'er the vaunt and firstlings of those broils,
> Beginning *in the middle.*

'Could it be that this too is a pun? Modern lawyers refer to Inner and
Middle without the addition of Temple.'[7] So 'in the middle' means 'here'.
Shakespeare never despised an easy laugh.

Middle Temple Hall.
Courtesy of the Honourable Society of the Middle Temple.

It seems obvious that Shakespeare was at home with his Middle Temple audience, as they with him, and that this implies a degree of familiarity, an ongoing social relationship. It might well have been nurtured at the Mermaid Tavern, by St Paul's, which was a meeting place for literary men as well as lawyers. There was an immensely strong tradition of literary involvement at the Middle Temple. Dramatists who were Middle Temple men included John Webster, John Marston and John Ford. (Francis Beaumont was Inner Temple.) No one disputes that in 1602 the Middle Temple was at the heart of the London literary scene.

The staging of *Twelfth Night* would have taken full advantage of the Hall. One enters the Hall through one of two large doorways. These would have been the indispensable entrances to the acting space, stage right and stage left. There's a gallery above the entrances, which in theory might have been used as the upper stage (balcony in *Romeo and Juliet*, Harfleur wall in *Henry V*). But there's too much wood panelling fronting the gallery for the audience to get much of a view of the players, and anyway *Twelfth Night* does not call for an upper stage scene. T. J. King, analysing the stage directions in *Twelfth Night*, shows that they would fit a simple stage with two entrances at the rear.[8] The directions include '*within*' but not '*above*'. The gallery is there for the minstrels.

I can't altogether go along with Arlidge on the staging. He believes that a stage was erected after the dinner and before the performance. This would be cumbersome and awkward, and I see no real gain. Actors would have to mount up the rear steps to get on to the stage, not an ideal entrance. The audience would remain at ground level, no rake being possible. Arlidge reckons that 'It is most unlikely that scaffolding would have been erected in the Middle Temple Hall [i.e."degrees", placed against the walls]. The audience would in any event have been seated on benches.'[9] Only grudgingly, and without elaboration, does he arrive at what I believe to be the main line of performance: 'Another possibility would have been to clear away some of the dining tables and place the remaining seating in a horse-shoe shape, allowing the screen to be used as a backdrop.'[10] That is simplicity and effectiveness itself. Why not accept Peter Brook's 'empty space' as the governing principle of performance, and assume that the actors simply came in through the two entrances to play on a cleared space?

It all sounds like dinner theatre. A lavish feast is laid on for the worthies of the Middle Temple, with benches and tables set in the Hall. A signal is given, and the assembly breaks up, to explore the comfort zones and to see if the technology is as advanced as the glass. When people return, they find that the benches are now arranged in a horseshoe facing the main entrances. They settle themselves along the benches – the tables have been cleared away – those close to the action being reserved for the Temple magnificos. Music is playing, up on the gallery. Orsino and his followers enter. 'If music be the food of *love*' – a courtly bow here to the Prince of Love – 'play on,' and the audience applauds the compliment. They will also register 'that surfeiting, / The appetite may sicken, and so die', which speaks directly to their condition. The lawyers settle down on their benches. 'Enough, no more, / 'Tis not so sweet now as it was before,' and Orsino signals to the gallery. The minstrels fall silent. So do the watchers.

Everything is a stage direction. The audience can now concentrate on 'O spirit of *love*', which drains a final, residual half-laugh from the audience. *Twelfth Night*, it may be for the first time, has properly begun.

The Treasurer got his wish. Next year, under James I, he was appointed Serjeant. I reckon he earned it.

Notes

1.   Leslie Hotson, *The First Night of 'Twelfth Night'* (Rupert Hart-Davis, 1954).

2.   Anthony Arlidge, *Shakespeare and the Prince of Love: The Feast of Misrule in the Middle Temple* (Giles de la Mare, 2000).

3.   Arlidge, *Shakespeare and the Prince of Love*, p. 3.

4.   The splendid portraits are reproduced, for example, in the catalogue to the Van Dyck exhibition at the Royal Academy of Arts in September–December 1999 (published by Royal Academy Publications and Antwerpen Open). The editors, Christopher Brown and Hans Vlieghe, list the subjects' names as 'Shirley' (p. 160).

5.   Arlidge, *Shakespeare and the Prince of Love*, p. 27.

6.   Arlidge, *Shakespeare and the Prince of Love*, p. 116.

7.   Arlidge, *Shakespeare and the Prince of Love*, p. 111.

8.   T. J. King, *Shakespearean Staging 1599–1642* (Harvard University Press, 1971).

9.   Arlidge, *Shakespeare and the Prince of Love*, p. 120.

10. Arlidge, *Shakespeare and the Prince of Love*, p. 121.

four

HADDON HALL AND THE CATHOLIC NETWORK

IF anything can change our understanding of Shakespeare's life, it is likely to be a massive research project that has gained momentum of recent years. The usual shorthand for this project is 'Shakespeare's Lancashire Connection', stemming from E. A. J. Honigmann's brilliant *Shakespeare: The 'Lost Years'*.[1] I prefer to think of it as 'the Catholic network'. It all centres on one big fact (which is itself ambivalent) and a

Haddon Hall.
Courtesy of Haddon Hall, Bakewell.

myriad of smaller facts, which, like tiny fish, seem to point the same way as the large pilot fish.

Baptism, marriage licence and the christening of his children aside, we know nothing of Shakespeare's life until September 1592, when Robert Greene attacked him in print. Shakespeare was then twenty-eight. What was he doing during those 'lost years'? The antiquary John Aubrey, writing in the seventeenth century, cited a report that Shakespeare 'had been in his younger years a schoolmaster in the country'. But there was no confirmation, and the matter remained uncertain for centuries.

Now for the big fact, first mooted by Oliver Baker and taken up by Sir Edmund Chambers. In August 1581 Alexander Hoghton, a gentle-man of Lea (in Lancashire) made his will. In it he bequeathed his stock of play clothes and all his musical instruments to his brother Thomas, or, if he did not choose to keep players, to Sir Thomas Hesketh, and added: 'And I most heartily require the said Sir Thomas to be friendly unto Fulk Gyllome and William Shakeshafte now dwelling with me and either to take them unto his service or else to help them to some good master, as my trust is he will.'[2] Hoghton also provided annuities for eleven of his servants. Fulk Gyllome and William Shakeshafte each got forty shillings. Could this 'Shakeshafte' be Shakespeare? He could indeed.

Names were not thought of as fixed and unalterable in that era. Marlowe is referred to in contemporary accounts as Marley, Morley, Marlin. Chambers, the foremost Shakespearean scholar of the early twentieth century, lists a staggering eighty-three spelling variants of 'Shakespeare' in his monumental *William Shakespeare: A Study of Facts and Problems*.[3] He goes on to remark that 'Richard Shakespeare clearly appears in the Snitterfield court rolls as both Shakeschafte and Shakstaff'.[4] To my mind, the most significant variant comes in the Revels accounts of 1604–5, the official records of court performances. Several plays by Shakespeare were performed, including *The Merchant of Venice*, *The Comedy of Errors* and *Measure for Measure*. In each case the 'poet' is given as 'Shaxberd.' Here is the most successful court dramatist at the height of his fame, clearly the favourite of King James himself—who ordered a repeat performance of *The Merchant of Venice* two days after the first – and yet the court officials failed to get his name right (to our way of thinking). Moreover, the name 'Shakespeare' had appeared on the title page of a number of plays, published as quartos. If Shakespeare could be 'Shaxberd' to the court, he could be 'Shakeshafte' to Alexander Hoghton.

There is also the possibility that in a dangerous era Shakespeare may have felt it desirable to be a little less than precise about his name. 'Shakeshafte', a common name, is not an alias but could foster some confusion. Besides, a later age is accustomed to having actors vary their birth name somewhat. We might see his Hoghton name as a 'tweaking' of 'Shakespeare'. What follows? Honigmann says rightly that we need a scenario to account for the identification: 'how does a gifted youth from provincial Stratford, without a university degree, find employment as a schoolmaster?' He goes on:

> The obvious answer is that he must have been recommended as capable of the work of a schoolmaster, or assistant master, even though he had no degree. Anyone in Stratford could have recommended him, but one person in particular would have been an invaluable referee: the schoolmaster at Stratford's grammar school, who would be able to give an expert opinion of young Shakespeare's scholarly attainments.[5]

That seems highly plausible. Shakespeare, though we have no documentary proof, must surely have studied at King Edward VI Grammar School. Now comes the breakthrough. The schoolmaster at KES during Shakespeare's mid-teens was John Cottom, an Oxford graduate, who held the post from 1579 to 1581 or 1582. Cottom returned in 1582 to Tarnacre, in Lancashire, where his family owned property. Tarnacre is ten miles from Lea. This looks like more than coincidence; and then Honigmann discovered that one of the legatees in Hoghton's will was one John Cotham, who might well have been the teacher from Stratford.

Assume the link as given, and the underlying story comes out plain. The Hoghton family had strong Catholic sympathies. Lancashire was a hotbed of Catholicism. John Cottom was the brother of the Catholic priest Thomas Cottam, who was captured by the authorities and executed as a traitor in 1582. Shakespeare himself may well have come from a Catholic family. It is in the nature of things that external evidence should be meagre, for Catholics were persecuted and tried to keep their religion a secret. The Spiritual Testament of John Shakespeare, William's father, proves him a Catholic; the document no longer exists but its implication is generally accepted that William was brought up in a covertly Catholic household.[6] And an Anglican clergyman, at the end of the seventeenth century, wrote that Shakespeare had 'died a papist'.

I stress the difficulties for Catholics under Elizabeth's reign. The Act of Supremacy (1559) established the Church of England as the state religion. Those who rejected its outward forms and practices were fined, or worse. And yet Catholicism had been the state religion until 1558. Nearly two hundred Catholics were executed during Elizabeth's reign. So it is highly unlikely that the Hoghton family would employ at a time so dangerous for recusants a servant who was not a practising Catholic. Young Shakespeare was 'safe', and John Cottom had every reason for assuring himself, and his patron, on the point. As for the nature of the work, it could easily have combined some academic duties – teaching the children of the household, say, as Andrew Marvell did for Sir Thomas Fairfax at Nun Appleton House – with theatricals. 'Players' were then understood to comprise 'singers' and 'instrumentalists'. They were all-round entertainers. Hoghton's phrase, 'and all manner of play-clothes', suggests a varied stock of theatrical costumes. All in all, it sounds like an ideal first job for a promising young man.

Honigmann's reconstruction of events goes like this:

> John Cottom, recently arrived in Stratford as the new schoolmaster, hears that a Lancashire magnate, landlord to Cottom's own father and a near neighbour of his, needs a master to teach the children in his large household. Cottom recommends William Shakespeare, a brilliant boy of sixteen or so whose father is going through hard times. On his arrival the new schoolmaster, an admirer of Terence and Plautus, quickly teams up with Hoghton's players, and so impresses Hoghton that a career in 'playing', rather than as an unqualified schoolmaster, seems the obvious way forward.[7]

This is most convincing. As Honigmann says, 'If simple Mr Yates could carry all before him at Mansfield Park, what might not a brilliant young schoolmaster have achieved at Hoghton Tower?'[8]

There's some evidence, including family tradition, that Shakespeare and Fulk Gyllome followed the will's provisions – for Alexander Hoghton died that August – and went to Sir Thomas Hesketh of Rufford. Rufford is a dozen miles away from Hoghton Tower. The Rufford connection surfaces years later, when Thomas Savage, a London goldsmith, acted as trustee for Shakespeare and four colleagues in the building of the Globe. Savage was a native of Rufford. As Leslie Hotson says, for Shakespeare to choose a trustee from Rufford – 'a speck on the map more than two hundred road-miles from London' – and a man related to the Rufford Heskeths by marriage, makes the identification of Shakespeare/Shakeshafte look decidedly interesting.

The road from Rufford lay north. The Heskeths were on intimate terms with Henry Stanley, fourth Earl of Derby, whose country seat was Knowsley Hall (six miles east of Liverpool). The Stanleys were the largest landowners in Lancashire. The Earl of Derby and his eldest son, Lord Strange, kept a famous troupe of players, eight of whom were to form in 1594 the nucleus of the Lord Chamberlain's Men. That was Shakespeare's company. There is conjecture, but no proof, that Shakespeare had been a minor member of the old Strange's (Derby's) Men. In 1592 Strange's Men had played in London at the Rose, a repertory that included '*Harey the Vj*', probably Shakespeare's *Henry VI*, Part One. Shakespeare, socially adroit and professionally gifted, would have been well placed to make the big career move into the Chamberlain's Men. Overall, it is likely that Sir Thomas Hesketh looked after the young man entrusted to him in his friend's will, and passed him on to the household of a greater and more theatrically influential family. The Lancashire connection moves on to become, through the Earl of Derby, the staple of Shakespeare's sojourn in the north.

That takes us into the more accessible period of Shakespeare's life. The main thesis is this: Shakespeare got early on to a network, as ambitious and talented young people do. This network was a tight circle of aristocratic Catholicism. Later on, the evidence takes on the quality and substance of Shakespeare's early plays – the role of the Earl of Derby in *Richard III*, for example. Derby in that play holds the vital 'swing' role, the nobleman who turns against the tyrant and brings the land to Tudor rule. And the title page of *Titus Andronicus* (1594) states that it was 'Plaide by the Right Honourable the Earle of Darbie, Earle of Pembrooke, and Earle of Sussex their Servants'. But broadly, the argument goes forward on a host of linkages, minor people who turn up again and again in juxtapositions that go far beyond 'coincidence'.

Everything is buttressed by the body of work on the continuing relevance of Catholicism to English culture. Two recent books stake out a deal of scholarly positioning.[9] They offer accumulating evidence of Shakespeare's Catholicism, and of the soil from which it sprang. 'Shakespeare's signature ambiguity came from the collision of his Catholic context with his need to conform to "national feeling",' says Richard Wilson.[10] There is now a solidly researched foundation for Shakespeare's Catholic background, and thus the main support for his early travels in Lancashire – and perhaps the adjacent county of the Earl's title, Derbyshire.

The Derbyshire connection is worth exploring. It must have included some physical contexts, could we but see them. We know, for example, that the Queen's Men played at Chatsworth in 1593. Pembroke's Men played at Hardwick Hall in 1600, as had Chandos's Players in 1595, among them Robert Armin, who was later Shakespeare's colleague in the Chamberlain's/King's Men.

I'll propose a possibility from Shakespeare's early career. I have had the pleasure of visiting Haddon Hall in Derbyshire, 'the most perfect English house to survive from the Middle Ages', says Simon Jenkins,[11] and am deeply taken with its possibilities as the setting for an open-air theatrical production. That is because its salient feature is the 'base court' – the Lower Courtyard – and the flights of steps leading down to it, visibly, from the battlements. Since Haddon's base court is raked, the upper end makes a perfect 'upper stage'. The Earl of Worcester's Men, under one Hammond, had played at Haddon Hall in 1565.[12] Any Shakespearean must at once think of *Richard II* and the Act III scene in which Richard comes down from the battlements to speak directly with Bolingbroke on the base court.

Northumberland   My lord, in the base court he doth attend
To speak with you, may it please you to come
down. (3.3.176-7)

Two views of Haddon Hall, base court.
Courtesy of Haddon Hall, Bakewell.

And Richard, after a minor cadenza on the symbolic meaning of 'base', comes down to the base court. Haddon Hall is the perfect setting. The 'King' has only to descend the steps from the walls, in full view of the audience, and make his way on to the courtyard. The *mise-en-scène* is entirely compatible with the other scenes in the play. Is it possible that Shakespeare had a personal connection with Haddon Hall, and envisaged it as the frame for the play he had in mind?

I think it is. The nominal setting for the base court scene in *Richard II* is Flint Castle in Flintshire. There is however no evidence or likelihood that Shakespeare ever travelled that far west; it was not on the touring companies' map. But there is a strong case that Shakespeare as a young man saw something of the north of England, through his noble connections. If one accepts E. A. J. Honigmann's argument, as I do, then Shakespeare started his career at Hoghton Hall before moving on to patrons who included Lord Strange, later Earl of Derby. There is an obvious suggestion that 'Ferdinand', King of Navarre in *Love's Labour's Lost*, is a good-humoured nod to Ferdinando Stanley, Lord Strange. Honigmann puts forward persuasive dramatic evidence that Shakespeare wrote parts of *Love's Labour's Lost* and *Richard III* to flatter, or appeal to, Ferdinando Stanley. It is no great leap to suppose that Shakespeare travelled beyond the Lancashire county border and visited Haddon Hall, in company with his patron, during this period.

This means a relationship with the Vernon and Rutland families, great Catholic names, linked by marriage since 1563. In the garden at Haddon is a topiary hedge, clipped to display a boar's head and a peacock, emblems of Vernon and Manners. Haddon Hall is still owned by the Manners family, Dukes of Rutland. Such evidence as the plays afford suggests that Shakespeare was on good terms with them. The many references to young Rutland in *Henry VI*, Part Three, are compassionate and sympathetic. Aumerle, Earl of Rutland, is a favourable role in *Richard II*. Sir Richard Vernon comes well out of *Henry IV*, Part One. He is given a magnificent speech in Act IV, scene 1, well beyond the needs of the scene. A recent editor notes that Vernon's part has been 'substantially augmented' from Holinshed. May it not be true that 'Vernon' in *Henry IV*, Part One, is Shakespeare's way of saying 'Thank you' to his host?

It is certain that Shakespeare was on excellent terms with the sixth Earl of Rutland in 1613, for the Earl's steward recorded payment of 44s. 'to Mr Shakespeare in gold about my lord's impresa'. The impresa was an allegorical device, made to be borne by the Earl at a tournament on the king's Accession Day, 24 March 1613. It is reasonable to infer a long-term relationship between Shakespeare, the Rutlands and the Vernons.

This does not, of course, imply tolerance of an outer anti-Stratfordian heresy. The thesis that the Earl of Rutland wrote Shakespeare's plays was argued by Peter Porovshikov (*Shakespeare Unmasked*) and Claude W. Sykes (*Alias William Shakespeare*). They were barking up a tree next to

Steps outside Haddon Hall.
Courtesy of Haddon Hall, Bakewell.

the right one. I see no difficulty with the proposition that Shakespeare was acquainted with Roger Manners, fifth Earl of Rutland (1576–1612). The Earl had travelled on the Continent in 1595–6, and had studied for a while in Padua. He was briefly imprisoned in the Tower over the Essex plot. Another conspirator, the Earl of Southampton, Shakespeare's patron, had married Elizabeth Vernon, the daughter of Sir John Vernon of Hodnet. Again we see linkages that are not decisive but cumulatively are highly suggestive.

At all events, the affinities between *Richard II* and the base court at Haddon Hall are manifest. Has Haddon Hall ever been the *mise-en-scène* for a performance? These days, the interest in historic venues for Shakespearean performances is growing. The Middle Temple Hall saw in 2004 a performance of *Twelfth Night* on 2 February, as it did on Candlemas 1602. The Middle Temple setting feeds into the text itself. The Shakespeare Globe company put on *Measure for Measure* at Hampton Court in 2004. Productions of *Hamlet* at Kronborg Castle in 2000 and 2001 gained enormously from the authentic setting. It seems to me plausible that Shakespeare had a personal acquaintance with Haddon Hall, and that this entered his imaginative conception of *Richard II* and its staging.

I have not been concerned here to make out the larger Catholic case for Shakespeare's religious affiliation. That case may not need to rest on what Peter Milward SJ called 'a convergence of probabilities'. The position taken by Roland Mushat Frye, that Shakespeare employed references to religious doctrine for his dramatic purposes, is to me satisfying, as it is to Maurice Hunt in his book *Shakespeare's Religious Allusiveness: Its Play and Tolerance*.[12] He argues that Shakespeare integrates Protestant and Catholic motifs and systems of thought. My interest is narrower. For me, the Catholic connection offers a scenario that accounts for much of Shakespeare's early career. Accept it, and what has been in darkness yields at least its contours to the fitful probings of an imperfect searchlight.

The Shakeshafte link is destined to become ever more important as a generator of research. The Hoghton Tower Shakespeare Centre, a large-scale complex development, is now being planned. Its academic sponsor is the University of Lancaster. Shakespeare's Lancashire Connection is set to grow.

Notes

1.   E. A. J. Honigmann, *Shakespeare: The 'Lost Years'* (Manchester University Press, 1985).

2.   Honigmann, *Shakespeare: The 'Lost Years'*, p. 3.

3.   E. K. Chambers, *William Shakespeare: A Study of Facts and Problems*, 2 vols (Clarendon Press, 1930), vol. II, p. 371.

4.   Chambers, *William Shakespeare: A Study of Facts and Problems*, p. 372.

5.   Honigmann, *Shakespeare: The 'Lost Years'*, p. 5.

6.   Dennis Taylor, 'Bearish on the Will: John Shakespeare in the Rafters', *The Shakespeare Newsletter* (Spring 2004).

7.   Honigmann, *Shakespeare: The 'Lost Years'*, p. 21.

8.   Honigmann, *Shakespeare: The 'Lost Years'*, p. 28.

9.   Richard Dutton, Alison Findlay and Richard Wilson (eds), *Region, Religion, and Patronage: Lancastrian Shakespeare* (Manchester University Press, 2003); Richard Dutton, Alison Findlay and Richard Wilson (eds), *Theatre and Religion: Lancastrian Shakespeare* (Manchester University Press, 2003).

10.   Richard Dutton, 'Introduction: a torturing hour—Shakespeare among the martyrs', in Dutton, Findlay and Wilson, *Theatre and Religion*.

11.   Simon Jenkins, *England's Thousand Best Houses* (Allen Lane, 2003).

12.   Roland Mushat Frye, *Shakespeare and Christian Doctrine* (Princeton University Press, 196); Maurice Hunt, *Shakespeare's Religious Allusiveness: Its Play and Tolerance* (Ashgate, 2004).

five

EPHESUS AND *THE COMEDY OF ERRORS*

SHAKESPEARE never saw Ephesus. It is as certain as anything can be that he never left England, save just possibly on tour if his company crossed the border to Wales (they certainly performed in Ludlow). Nobody went to Scotland, until Jonson performed his celebrated, much-advertised walk to Edinburgh in 1618. Ireland was *terra incognita*, and for good reasons. English actors, three of them Shakespeare's own colleagues, did indeed travel on the Continent, but Will Kemp appears

Theatre in Ephesus, Turkey.
Courtesy of the Embassy of the Republic of Turkey,
Office of the Counsellor for Culture and Information.

to have been the only actor of his era to have travelled to Italy. Thomas Nashe links Kemp's name with Bergamo, in northern Italy, and there is a company in-joke in *A Midsummer Night's Dream*. Bottom (played by Kemp) offers to play the Duke 'a Bergamask dance between two of our Company' – this is the sole citation for 'bergomask' in the *OED* – and Theseus politely declines. We can surmise that Kemp, the archetypal travel bore, had already delighted the company long enough with his cultural speciality, a folk dance imported from Bergamo. At all events, foreign travel for Elizabethan actors was rarely attempted, dangerous and ill-rewarded. Ephesus, in what is now Turkey, was a world away from the experience of the English stage.

And yet the impress of that location is very strong in *The Comedy of Errors*. Shakespeare had an uncanny faculty for extracting from his sources a sense of the *genius loci*. Everything starts in its setting, Ephesus, and the town seems to vibrate in the text. A long footnote in Standish Hennings's Variorum Edition (2011) concludes that the sixteenth-century history of Ephesus is almost blank. For the Elizabethans, though, the local associations of Ephesus would mean something. They thought of it as a great seaport, renowned for its Temple of Diana. St Paul stayed there for two years. Hence the audience would connect it with St Paul's Epistle to the Ephesians and its appeals for domestic unity. That bears upon the marital strife of Antipholus of Ephesus and Adriana. They would also remember that Ephesus was known for sorcerers and exorcists, and for St Paul's 'curious arts':

> They say this town is full of cozenage,
> As nimble jugglers that deceive the eye,
> Dark-working sorcerers that change the mind,
> Soul-killing witches that deform the body,
> Disguised cheaters, prating mountebanks ...
> And many such-like liberties of sin. (1.2.97–102)

The biblical allusions help to establish the dark underside of the play. But these cultural referents are absorbed in the broad symbolism of the action and its background, with the atavistic appeal to collective memories of wandering and loss. Always at the back of the action is the sea, as great a presence here as in *The Tempest*. It is the sea that parts Egeon from his family, that brings Antipholus of Syracuse to Ephesus, that calls him throughout, 'For he is bound to sea, and stays but for it' (4.1.33); 'Both wind and tide stays for this gentleman' (4.1.46). That sense of the sea – waiting, pulling, imperious – is strong in *The Comedy of Errors*. The great Harbour Road is still there, leading from the theatre to the sea. But it goes nowhere, for the sea has moved three miles away.

We tend to think of coastal erosion as a problem, but the process works the other way too, and river siltings have reclaimed much of the sea in the region. (The river Maeander gave the word 'meander' to the English language.) Along the Harbour Road one can imagine Antipholus of Syracuse strolling aimlessly, 'I will go lose myself, / And wander up and down to see the city' (1.2.30–1).

That city is preserved into the unity of time and place, for the action takes place within Ephesus and within one day. The named locations are the 'street' or 'mart', the 'house' of Antipholus of Ephesus, called the Phoenix, the 'house' of the Courtesan, called the Porpentine, and the Priory which houses the Abbess. Trevor Nunn's notable production for the RSC (1976) made use of the upper stage or minstrels' gallery for the upper floor of the house on which Adriana appears, taking the hint from 'Husband, I'll dine above with you today' (2.2.207). One stage direction is particularly interesting: at 4.1.85, '*Enter Dromio Sira, from the Bay*'. This looks like the author's direction. It suggests that Shakespeare had in mind Plautus' *Menaechmi* and *Amphitruo* – these were popular grammar school texts, and it is likely that Shakespeare read them in the fourth form. In Plautus, one side of the stage leads to the city, the other side to the bay or harbour. The deep imprint of these situations is evident all through the key passages. The essential fact is that the setting for *The Comedy of Errors* is imagined as a *sea*port, not just nominally but as the existential setting.

The city's economy is mercantile, driven by the community leaders and their agreed goals. 'Universal, immutable, impartial', said De Gaulle of gold. It is the international currency of drama, too, and is everywhere in *The Comedy of Errors*. The chain, the ring, 500 ducats, 1,000 marks, guilders, angels – *gold* pieces are the props of this play. And they define the play's society. Our impressions of Ephesus may be hazy – it is a

Mediterranean seaport, characteristically studded with English taverns such as the Tiger, Centaur, Phoenix, Porpentine (and not so different from the Irish pubs everywhere today in Club Med resorts) – but our sense of its inhabitants is sharp. Topped by the Duke, tailed by the servants, Ephesan society is focused on its merchant class.

The businessmen, Antipholus of Ephesus, Balthazar, Angelo (a goldsmith), the First and Second Merchant, set the tone of the town. Ephesus is an international trading centre, and, like Venice, it is founded on political stability, the free movement of capital, effective border controls, reliable and equitable laws that the local judiciary may not adjust at whim. 'Now trust me, were it not against our laws, / ...Which Princes, would they, may not disannul' is Solinus's apology to Egeon (1.1.143–5). Venice, a greater city-state, has the same problem, for, as Antonio says,

> The Duke cannot deny the course of law;
> For the commodity that strangers have
> With us in Venice, if it be denied,
> Will much impeach the justice of the state,
> Since that the trade and profit of the city
> Consisteth of all nations. (*The Merchant of Venice*, 3.3.26–31)

Note too the alacrity with which the Ephesan gendarmerie backs up complaints of improper trading practices. Ephesus, when running smoothly, is designed for the frictionless accumulation of wealth. Its character-note is the First Merchant, regretfully declining a dinner invitation on the grounds that 'I am invited, sir, to certain merchants, / Of whom I hope to make much benefit' (1.2.24–5). A business engagement takes precedence over a purely social one, unless, like the Courtesan, who is able to diversify her business into supplying Antipholus with a diamond ring, she can happily combine the two. The action of *The Comedy of Errors* could not take place other than in a city whose business is business. Ephesus is run by the Rotarians.

The major feature of the city is, as it was in St Paul's time, the theatre. This is not precisely what we understand by 'theatre', a public building or space given over to theatrical performances. Such performances took place on only a handful of days in a year in classical times. This theatre is what we should term 'multi-purpose', and its main function was to hold public meetings.

It is in that light that we should consider the Ephesan theatre, with its magnificent semicircle of seats fanning upwards and outwards, rising far above the orchestra level (the semicircular space in front of the Greek theatre stage) and accommodating many thousands at its maximum. The uproarious town meeting there is described in Acts 19:24–9. What was the tumult all about? The problems arose when that 'Grand Disturber', St Paul, preached Christianity and came into conflict with the local business community. In the Bible's succinct and even-handed account, one Demetrius, a silversmith, organized a meeting of the craftsmen. Like him, they 'made silver shrines for Diana', which 'brought no small gain unto the craftsmen'. (Curiously enough, another Diana in our own times, the Princess of Wales, caused a bitter dispute between silversmiths and other makers of images. The modern silversmiths won their legal battle, for freedom to make images.) St Paul, according to Demetrius, turned people away from the craft and its customers, 'saying that they be no gods, which are made with hands'. His conclusion was fierce: 'So that not only this our craft is in danger to be set at naught; but also that the temple of the great goddess Diana should be despised, and her magnificence should be destroyed, whom all Asia and the world worshippeth'.

St Paul would have gone to the theatre, but his disciples dissuaded him. One of the advantages of being a disciple is that you get to have disciples, if you stay the course. The town clerk of Ephesus, a man of sterling good sense, brought order to a rowdy town meeting. He pointed out that Demetrius had a ready recourse. 'The law is open,' and a class action could be brought by Demetrius and his associates. 'But if ye enquire any thing concerning other matters, it shall be determined in a lawful assembly.' So the matter was defused, and issues of principle put off to a later date. St Paul left town immediately after, to save other parts of Asia

Demetrius had a case; the preachings of St Paul were damaging to the livelihood of the silversmiths' guild. Small wonder that the guild members organized a demonstration. 'And the whole city', we are told, 'was filled with confusion.' 'Confusion' is a fair capsule version of the plot of *The Comedy of Errors*, especially in the later stages, when the entire company is rushing around in search of a resolution to its enquiries. The guild power of the silversmiths, transposed to goldsmiths in this play, is evident in the action. Angelo opens Act V with a prolonged statement of his grievance, essentially a legal claim that has to be taken seriously by the highest in the land. Duke Solinus, who is exactly analogous to the Duke of Venice, must respect all forms of the law. He does, and rules in favour of the happy ending brought about by the Abbess.

The Priory, over which the Abbess reigns, is clearly a medical centre that has a strong line in marital counselling, as well as healing in general. This looks like a Shakespearean echo of a historic fact, that Ephesus, as the museum in neighbouring Selçuk tells us, was home to a large and respected medical school in Roman times. Rufus of Ephesus was one of the first doctors to widen his approach to psychiatry. Here is his prescription:

> The patient must be interviewed. By means of these questions it is possible to learn a great deal concerning the illness, which enables a better treatment. The time that an illness began is important. In addition one should enquire as to the patient's attitude towards life and general mental state. In this way the patient's mental health can be restored.

In *The Comedy of Errors* the 'doctor' figure who parallels the quack, Pinch, is the Abbess. Hers is a holistic approach to medicine. She comes on as one skilled in investigating the causes of 'possession' (unlike the charlatan Pinch, who also claims to treat 'possession'). She asks all the right questions of Adriana, starting with 'How long hath this possession held the man?' (5.1.44). Were there other causes of his mental state?

> Hath he not lost much wealth by wrack of sea?
> Buried some dear friend? Hath not else his eye
> Stray'd his affection in unlawful love,
> A sin prevailing much in youthful men,
> Who give their eyes the liberty of gazing?

Having sifted the evidence which Antipholus' wife supplies, the Abbess diagnoses (quite plausibly, if wrongly) the nature of his complaint. Adriana's railing, 'The venom clamours of a jealous woman', is judged to be the primary source of her husband's illness, and she admits that there may be something to it. That leads the Abbess to an acute analysis of the physical effects of emotional damage, 'Unquiet meals make ill digestion' (5.1.74). And:

> In food, in sport and life-preserving rest
> To be disturbed would mad or man or beast;
> The consequence is then, thy jealous fits
> Hath scared thy husband from the use of wits. (83–6)

This is pure Rufus of Ephesus doctrine.

The Abbess's recommended course of treatment is:

> He took this place for sanctuary,
> And it shall privilege him from your hands
> Till I have brought him to his wits again,
> Or lose my labour in assaying it …
> Be patient, for I will not let him stir
> Till I have used the approved means I have,
> With wholesome syrups, drugs, and holy prayers,
> To make of him a formal man again. (5.1.94–105)

If you wanted decent health care in ancient Ephesus, you went to the Abbess, not Pinch. Shakespeare must have got hold of the idea that there was an upside to the Ephesan health service, and that they got it from the renowned Rufus.

To a modern audience, Adriana may well be the most resonant character. Is she a lineal descendant of the Roman shrew, or a proto-modern Nora fretting at the bonds which society imposes on her? She accepts the Abbess's rulings and thus confirms her journey back to full mental well-being. And that is the play's final position, all relations being restored to harmony. In the fullest sense, Ephesus becomes a place of healing.

One comes away from Ephesus feeling that Shakespeare had made a shrewd assessment of the town's qualities. He would have been interested to note the lively entrepreneurial spirit in today's townsfolk, a tradition that survives effortlessly through the centuries. If the sea had stayed by Ephesus, so would the shore culture that Shakespeare depicts so vividly, and there is much more to this play than Acts 19. Every play of Shakespeare's contains its own society, its own world. *The Comedy of Errors* is no exception.

six

SHAKESPEARE'S VENICE

'Ah, good old Mantuan, I may speak of thee as the traveller doth of Venice: *Venetia, Venetia, Chi non ti vede, non ti pretia* . . . who understandeth thee not, loves thee not.'

(*Love's Labour's Lost*, 4.2.93–8)

Rialto Bridge, Venice.
© Kumar Sriskandan/Alamy

THUS the pedant Holofernes, combining two strokes of one-up-manship: all educated people know that Mantuanus, better known as Virgil, is a great writer, and all know that Venice is the place to see on one's Grand Tour. I have nothing to say about Mantuanus, whom I have neglected disgracefully. But the Grand Tour is now coming back, I note, as a shorthand ideal for travellers. And one can see traces of Shakespearean involvement in Venice.

Our idea of Venice is an image of decaying beauty. It is a nine-teenth-century idea, promoted by the great travellers of the era. Wherever Byron went, he turned out a canto for *Childe Harold* and his other poetic travelogues. For him, Venice was a symbol of republican freedom, now overthrown: 'Venice is crush'd' ('Ode to Venice'). Henry James saw gilded but passé beauty. I suppose we conjure up Thomas Mann's *Death in Venice*, the movie anyway, with its swelling Mahler soundtrack. The smell of decomposition lingers over the Venice memorialized for its sinister beauty.

And we have to strip all that away, like layers of paint, from the image of Venice that Shakespeare re-created in two plays. For him, Venice was a luminous success. Beauty scarcely entered into it. Venice was the code name for a successful commercial republic. It was also the free state of Europe, an ethnic and religious melting-pot. Standing on the eastern borders of Europe, Venice confronted the Turks. As William Shute, the English translator of the first history of Venice, put it, 'Italy is the face of Europe; Venice the eye of Italy. It is not only the fairest but the strongest and activest part of that beautiful and powerful nation.'

Shakespeare knew a great deal about the city. He would have encountered many signs of the tiger Venetian economy in England. Verzelini acquired a monopoly to make Venetian glass in London in 1575 – an early instance of the Italian export drive in designer products. A glance at the 'Venice' entry in the *Oxford English Dictionary* shows the extraordinary range of Venetian products that had entered the language in Shakespeare's day. 'Venice treacle' was used by pharmacists. 'Venetian gold' was cloth of gold, much employed in expensive finery. There was 'Venetian turpentine' and a 'Venetian beam'. All such imports were of high quality and priced accordingly. And everyone knew that the Venetian envoy was high on the list of diplomatic notables. Elizabeth I reproached the Venetian envoy for there not being a resident ambassador at her court; and this was done in the reign of her successor, James I. (We have an excellent account of London play-going in 1617, when the entire Venetian embassy went to the theatre and Chaplain Busino recorded his impressions. He was very taken with the fashionably-dressed courtesan who came and sat next to him.) The idea of the might and sagacity of the Venetian state was well current in Shakespeare's England.

For Shakespeare, Venice is the setting of *The Merchant of Venice* and the first act of *Othello*. He clearly knows a good deal about Venice and has assimilated his knowledge into the location-values of his two plays. There is a limited amount of local colour, detail designed to impress the audience with its show of authenticity. The contrast here is with Ben Jonson. His *Volpone* (1606, the year of *Macbeth*), set in Venice, is saturated with the sense of place. 'I, who was ever wont to fix my bank in face of the public Piazza, near the shelter of the Portico to the Procuratia...' (2.2.34–6) comes from Volpone's great mountebank address to the Venetian crowd, something which actually gains from being spoken with an Italian accent and rhythms. Beyond the local colour is the sense of location values. Jonson sees a city obsessed with money, in a way as much reflex as central. When Mosca, the supposed heir to Volpone's wealth enters the Scrutineo (the Venetian court of law), the immediate reaction of the 4th Avocatore (judge) is 'A proper man and, were Volpone dead, / A fit match for my daughter' (5.12.50–1).

Shakespeare knows very well that Venice is a great city-state, whose wealth is founded on commerce between East and West. He is fairly light on local detail. There is, for example, no mention of San Marco, the most famous piazza in Europe. The Rialto is mentioned several times, not as the bridge which it is today, but as the Exchange where 'gentlemen and merchants' do business together. This Exchange is presented as a centre of news-gathering and business (and not as a building with specific architectural features). 'What news on the Rialto?' is the key line – repeated (1.3.34, 3.1.1), always a sign that Shakespeare attaches importance to the point. Shylock shares the line with Solanio. It is on the Rialto that the disgraced Antonio cannot show his face. The Rialto is the nerve-centre of Shakespeare's Venice.

That perennial adjunct to Venetian life, the gondola, gets a key mention. It is one of those highly condensed, tight passages where Shakespeare is concerned to get a lot across in a short space. Following the flight of Jessica with Lorenzo, reports Solanio,

> The villain Jew with outcries raised the Duke,
> Who went with him to search Bassanio's ship.
> He came too late – the ship was under sail,
> But there the Duke was given to understand
> That in a gondola was seen together
> Lorenzo and his amorous Jessica.
> Besides, Antonio certified the Duke
> They were not with Bassanio on his ship. (2.8.4–11)

The gondola is the symbol of illicit love, as well as a picturesque detail in the scene. It is placed in a context of relationships and assumptions. Shylock has clout with the authorities. He may be socially undesirable, but he is too wealthy and important to be ignored. The Duke is put to considerable inconvenience in investigating Shylock's complaint, but essentially accepts Shylock's point of view, that elopements are bad and should be stopped.

What is the relationship between Shylock and the Duke (Doge), the civic leader? Since Venice is founded on wealth, it follows that the sanctity of money and contracts is the basic law. The main plot of *The Merchant of Venice* turns on the enforcement of a contract. Antonio plays the futures market and gets hit, badly. He has neither insured nor hedged, just diversified. He is well liked and the Duke does what he can to help. But a contract is a contract. As we have seen in Singapore, a city-state founded on commerce is absolutely committed to the law of contract – and to punishing malefactors who bring into disrepute the city's high standards. Shylock is a leading representative of Venice's financial community, and an indispensable source of credit to the state. He has to be taken seriously.

Which brings us to that aspect of the matter which is still architecturally visible, the quarter where Jews live in Venice. They still do. The word 'ghetto' actually originated in Venice, where the first one came into existence. 'Ghetto' means 'foundry', and it applied to the site of the first ghetto in Venice. In 1516 the Senate decided that all Jews in Venice should move to the Ghetto Nuovo, an urban islet with two access points that could be closed at night. This arrangement permitted the authorities to protect the Jews from violence and looting, and to impose an effective curfew on them. The Venetian authorities were relatively lenient towards the Jews by European standards, but they laid down a policy which combined protection and separation.

So *ghetto* symbolized the segregation of Jews in Venice, and gradually became a generic term used all over Europe. (And now, of course, used loosely to denote any quarter where a given group, including diplomatic, lives together.) Today in Venice one can still visit the Ghetto Vecchio and Ghetto Novissimo, and still feel the impress of architecture on the mind. Since the area for building was fixed and could not be expanded, the buildings had to reach up to the sky. They are tall for Venice, growing to six or more storeys. The windows tend to face inwards towards the square or open areas, not outward to the rest of Venice. 'The Ghetto turned a blind face to the city', wrote Mary McCarthy in *Venice Observed*. The overall effect of the Jewish Quarter is austere, closed-off, inward-looking, not without a sense of danger.

This is what caught the imagination of a distinguished Shylock, Ian McDiarmid. He played the role for the Royal Shakespeare Company in 1984, and tells of his preparations:

> Before rehearsals began, I went to Venice, where I had a wonderful time, and found one thing of use. In the Jewish quarter, Ghetto Nuovo, I was fascinated to see that all the windows looked inward towards the square. None looked outward to the city, and the sea beyond. So, I extrapolated, the Jew was not permitted to look outwards. He had no alternative but to look inwards. Light was shut out. He was left obsessively to contemplate the dark. Less metaphorically, inside were all his possessions. His house was itself, and also the sole repository of his property: his wealth ('the means whereby I live') and his daughter Jessica ('the prop/That doth sustain my house').[1]

That insight explains a great deal in *The Merchant of Venice*, especially the meaning of 'house' ('ghetto' does not appear in the text). House and land are security itself. Shylock's distrust of the sea comes out early: 'and then there is peril of waters, winds and rocks' (1.3.22). McDiarmid also accounts for Shylock's distaste for Christian intruders into the ghetto streets:

> What, are there masques? Hear you me, Jessica:
> Lock up my doors, and when you hear the drum
> And the vile squealing of the wry-necked fife,
> Clamber not you up to the casements then,
> Nor thrust your head into the public street
> To gaze on Christian fools with varnished faces;
> But stop my house's ears – I mean my casements ...
>
> (2.5.27–33)

This is historically quite correct. Christian revellers often took part in masques and street dancing in the Jewish quarter during the feast of Purim. To Shylock they are intruders, disturbers of his peace of mind. One feels this in the Ghetto Vechio. And the eternal solace? It is the synagogue, still there. 'Go, Tubal, and meet me at our synagogue, go, good Tubal, at our synagogue, good Tubal' (3.1.102–3).

Shakespeare has accurately assessed the *genius loci*, and its effect on the people who dwell there. Venice updates readily. When Jonathan Miller directed his classic *The Merchant of Venice* for the National Theatre in 1970 (a production available on video and easily the best account of the play), he was struck with some photographs of Venice taken by the Count of Primoli in the late nineteenth century. Miller thought Shakespeare's drama interestingly consistent with this new context, as Primoli preserved it, and accordingly instructed his designer, Julia Trevelyan Oman, to create nineteenth-century settings and costumes. And it worked wonderfully well. Florian's, that cafe in the Piazza San Marco, with its red plush and gilt, seemed the exact setting for the business talk of the Venetians in the opening scene. Shylock (the last great Shakespearean part that Laurence Olivier played) became a Rothschild banker, blackballed at the club. Venice remains what it always was, a city

that lauds beauty but throbs with commerce. It is the grand container for
The Merchant of Venice.

As for *Othello*, there are strong indications that Shakespeare knew very
well the background to the story. The plot he got directly from an Italian
author, Geraldi Cinthio. Kenneth Muir, the expert on Shakespeare's
sources, thought it probable that Shakespeare had even read Cinthio in
the original Italian. There is a phrase in the Quarto text, 'as acerb as the
colonquintida' (1.3.350) that is suggestive. The Italian original uses the
word '*acerbe*', so 'acerb' (of which there is no previous instance in English)
sounds like a direct reminiscence. The word must have seemed odd to the
Folio printer, for it is changed to 'bitter' there, and is retained by many
editors. Again, the puzzling reference at 2.1.25 can be explained as being
based on a knowledge of Italian. Most editors read 'A ship is here put in,
/ A Veronesa', which is absurd, because Verona is an inland city. 'Fitted
out in Verona' sounds implausible. But the Folio has 'Verenessa', which
should mean a type of ship. The Italian verb is '*verrinare*', meaning 'to
cut through', so that the noun 'Verenessa' could mean 'cutter' (once the
standard term for a small ship). I think we can take it that Shakespeare
had a fair reading knowledge of Italian.

Othello's Venice features gondolas, of course: Roderigo tells
Brabantio, Desdemona's father, that she has been 'Transported with no
worse nor better guard / But with a knave of common hire, a gondo-
lier' (1.1.125–6), from which one gleans that no well-brought-up young
lady should be seen unescorted in a gondola. (Jonson makes much the
same point in *Volpone*.) The editors have filled many column-inches on
Iago's instruction to Roderigo: 'Lead to the Sagittary [Sagittar] the
raised search' (for Othello; 1.1.158). It sounds like an inn, but no inn-
name of that type has survived. One scholar has proposed that 'Sagittar'
or 'Sagittary' refers to the Frezzeria, the street of the arrow-makers.
Some have suggested the Arsenale, the biggest group of buildings in
Venice, as the location, for there was indeed a group of four statues
before the Arsenale, one of them a centaur/archer. 'Arsenale' itself is too
vague a meeting-point, the walls being almost two miles in circumfer-
ence. My own guess is that Shakespeare had in mind an inn, hard by the
Arsenale gates, and thus likely enough to take a topographical feature
for its sign.

To turn from topography to the play, it is plain that Shakespeare assimilated Venetian culture to his story. The play turns on jealousy, and that jealousy has to be at least partly credible. How can this be done? Desdemona is chaste and virtuous. She comes, however, from a culture which has a distinctive set of sexual mores. Iago turns this to account when he says to Othello:

> I know our country disposition well:
> In Venice they do let God see the pranks
> They dare not show their husbands: their best conscience
> Is not to leave undone, but keep unknown. (3.3.205–8)

Iago is now an insider. He is explaining to a foreigner, who does not understand these matters fully, how things are arranged in Venice. There is a striking testimony to Iago that comes two centuries later, from Byron. In late 1816 Byron came to Venice, and took up lodgings with the Segatis in the Frezzeria. (That name again!) Soon he became the lover of Marianna Segati, wife to his landlord. He wrote to John Murray, his publisher, on 2 January 1817:

> The general state of morals here is much the same as in the Doge's time – a woman is virtuous (according to the code) who limits herself to her husband and one lover – those who have two or three more are a little *wild*; – but it is only those who are indiscriminately diffuse – and form a low connection – such as the Princess of Wales with her Courier (who by the way is made a Knight of Malta) who are considered as overstepping the modesty of marriage ... There is no convincing a woman here – that she is in the smallest degree deviating from the rule of right or the fitness of things – in having an 'Amoroso'. The great sin seems to lie in concealing it – or in having more than one – that is – unless such an extension of the prerogative is understood and approved of by the prior claimant.

Byron was fairly sure that Marianna's husband knew about the liaison, but there was no clash or confrontation. It was simply a matter of keeping up appearances, and behaving according to a code that all Venetians understood. And as Byron says, I suppose rightly, things had not changed much since the Doge's time.

Othello is an outsider, an instrument of the state valued for his military prowess but not truly assimilated into Venetian ways of thought. He is a *condottiere*, a soldier of fortune like Bartolommeo Colleoni, whose statue by Verrocchio still stands in the square bearing his name. It is a marvellous image of power and movement, of obdurate masculinity, one of the greatest equestrian statues in the world. Even so, the Venetian authorities tricked Colleoni on its location. He wanted the Piazza San Marco, and got, after his death, a much more obscure setting. The Venetians were cool, hard-headed employers. They understood Othello pretty well, and 1.3 shows the Doge handling a tricky situation adroitly. Othello did not understand them at all well.

There is no evidence that Shakespeare ever visited Venice, or indeed left England. But he gleaned a great deal, picked up perhaps from Emilia Bassano, if A. L. Rowse is right in making her the Dark Lady of the Sonnets. Jonathan Bate's suggestion, that the Dark Lady is the wife of John Florio, retains the Italian connection. Florio was a translator and lexicographer, born in England of Italian parents, who may well have known Shakespeare. The city's values and topography are assimilated into the playwright's imaginative reconstructions: we can still recognize our Venice in Shakespeare's.

Notes

1.   Russell Jackson and Robert Smallwood (eds), *Players of Shakespeare 2* (Cambridge University Press, 1989), p. 48.

seven

HAMPTON COURT PALACE AND WHITEHALL

HAMPTON Court Palace saw the first Christmas revels of James's reign. Whitehall Palace was ruled out because of the plague, so the court travelled some twenty miles upstream to Hampton Court. There, from 26 December 1603 on, the season of plays unfolded. These were performed by Shakespeare's company, the King's Men, whose new title replaced the Chamberlain's Men soon after James had arrived in London from Edinburgh. We have the dates of the Hampton Court

Hampton Court Palace.
© Historic Royal Palaces. Photograph: James Brittain.

performances, but with a single exception no title. 'On New Year's night', wrote Sir Dudley Carleton, 'we had a play of Robin Goodfellow,' evidently *A Midsummer Night's Dream*. However, the authority on the subject, Alvin Kernan in *Shakespeare: The King's Playwright* (Yale University Press, 1995), argues powerfully that the play which King James saw performed in his presence on 26 December, St Stephen's Night, must have been *Hamlet*.

There are excellent reasons to accept *Hamlet* as the likely choice to open the season, on the first night after Christmas. The play was of course famous, as always. Five versions were played in Shakespeare's own era: the lost Ur-*Hamlet*, the First ('Bad') Quarto of 1603, the Second ('Good') Quarto (1604–5), the Folio (1623), and *Der Bestrafte Brudermord*, a degenerate German touring text. And the play was well designed to tickle the royal fancy. *Hamlet* is set in 'Elsinore', that is, Kronborg Castle, Helsingør. James had actually honeymooned there after his marriage to Anne of Denmark in 1590, and the royal couple had been forced to wait in Kronborg for months for a favourable wind from Denmark to Scotland. The play's action contains some piquancies, as when Claudius and Gertrude see the play-within-the-play performed – just as James and Anne look on at Claudius and Gertrude. The genuine royals have the best seats, for all to behold, while they contemplate the play royals. 'Hamlet performs the major functions of the Master of the Revels when he greets the players' (Kernan, *Shakespeare*, p. 13). Though *Hamlet* is a tragedy of state, there is no hint of too close a reference to current politics. Oblique comment is the key to the court plays. It was out of bounds to represent a living monarch or his undisguised interests. Those limits respected, that first court performance of *Hamlet* must have been a deeply engaging and satisfying experience for its audience. Since the play was *not* put on for the Christmas revels in the following year, 1604–5, the clear inference is that James had already seen it, at Hampton Court.

I can add an extra point to Kernan's argument. It used to be thought that there were six copies only of the Second Quarto in existence, evenly divided between England and the USA. In 1959 a seventh copy turned up, in excellent condition, in Warsaw public library (*Shakespeare Quarterly*, 11 (1960), 497.) It is now at the University of

Wroclaw, and was likely bought by a Polish traveller in England who had heard of an important new play with a substantial Polish content. Who could this traveller have been? The obvious candidate is the Polish ambassador. Kernan records a letter of Arbella Stuart in which she says that the Queen had arrived in Hampton Court on the sixteenth and that 'the King will be here tomorrow. The Polonian Imbassador shall have Audience on Thursday next' (*Shakespeare*, p. 28). He would have seen the play put on for the court and the distinguished visitors, and probably told one of his entourage to go out and buy the paperback of *Hamlet*. And that, I suggest, is how the Second Quarto started on its long journey to Poland.

Hampton Court contains the only surviving Tudor theatre, the Great Hall. Performances were in three places: the Great Hall, the Great Watching Chamber and the smaller Presence Chamber. It is clear that the Great Hall must have been the space where the action was mounted: it was the appropriate venue before the king himself. As the largest space, it could accommodate the largest audience. This was considerable. The entire court had come down to Hampton Court, besides great numbers of the diplomatic corps and their followers. Robert Cecil, Earl of Salisbury, complained to Shrewsbury on 23 December 1603, 'Other stuff I can send yow none from this place, wheare now we are to feast seven Embassadors; Spain, France, Poland, Florence, and Savoy ...' (Kernan, *Shakespeare*, p. 29). Continental nations had sent in their ambassadors to pay their respects to the new king, and this imposed a huge strain on the resources of Hampton Court, vast though the number of chambers was. (To this day, many of these chambers lie empty. Some fifty used to be grace-and-favour residences, but this practice has now been stopped, following a disastrous fire begun through the negligence of an elderly resident who perished in the flames. These residents at the most recent count were down to two. Dr Lucy Worsley, the chief curator at Historic Royal Palaces, has spoken of plans to make rooms into commercially let apartments.) Tents were set up in the park to accommodate the great numbers of visitors and their staff. All the court visitors regarded a place at the staging of the plays as essential to their own, and their country's, self-esteem and reputation. When Macbeth says at his banquet, 'You know your own degrees – sit down' (3.4.1), he means they know their rank and order of precedence. Shakespeare suggests that the guests sat down on benches, where they would have to know their place; rank was a determinant of seating. (This can sometimes become an issue on the House of Commons benches.) We know that at Whitehall the scramble for precedence among the courtiers was intense; it cannot have been less at Hampton Court.

We can get a flavour of the playing decisions from the actual performances of *Measure for Measure* that were staged in Hampton Court in 2004. This was a commercial enterprise which did not attempt to re-create the experience of a piece of court theatre. It was not a curatorial event. Brett Dolman, curator of collections at Hampton Court Palace, reports: 'We installed racked modern seating in the Tudor Great Hall and the only real nod to historic performance was the use that the actors made of the entrances underneath the Minstrels' Gallery at one end of the Hall' (letter to author). For the 2004 *Measure for Measure*, the authorities had removed the tapestries on the walls. Those same tapestries, for the 1603 performance of *Hamlet*, would have been a striking stage prop for the killing of Polonius. Dolman goes on:

> What we did do was to allow the actors to use the Great Watching Chamber as their pre-performance dressing space, which was interesting for our afternoon visitors, but which would not have happened historically. This end of the Hall was very much the royal space, as it linked the Great Hall to the royal apartments and allowed for the entrance and exit of the King (and family) to watch the play on a raised stage at the opposite end of the Hall to the actors.

Even these changes in a contemporary production tell us what Shakespeare must have observed, as one of the players in the Great Hall before the king and queen.

The 1604 season closed with Samuel Daniel's Twelfth Night masque, *The Vision of the Twelve Goddesses*, in which Queen Anne herself starred as Pallas Athena, coming down from the mountain erected at the screen end of the Great Hall. The more traditional members of the audience were mildly scandalized at the shortness of the queen's dress, which reached little below her knees. By then the King's Men had already packed their costumes and were off to perform on 6 January in Maldon, Essex, leaving the king and Council to finish off the festivities and to prepare for the great Hampton Court Conference shortly to come. The company was back in Hampton Court to play before the Florentine ambassador on Candlemas, 2 February, soon after which the court left for Whitehall, the regular scene of royal command performances over the next few years.

The King's Men were not back at Hampton Court till 7 August 1606, when a play was performed as part of the farewell for the Danish king, Christian IV. It was almost certainly *Macbeth*, a play which dramatizes the Stuart myth (as *Richard III* and *Henry VIII* dramatize and glorify the Tudor dynasty). What the stained-glass windows of Hampton Court did for the Tudors, those same windows in the Great Hall did for the Stuarts, as they glowed upon the royal scene. '*A shew of eight Kings, [the eighth] with a glass in his hand, and Banquo last*' is the Act IV, scene 1 stage direction: it is a living family tree that parades down time. The glass must surely have been tilted to reflect the face of James, yards away, as he watches the images of his predecessors. This is ancestor worship that bows to the highest purposes of state. *Macbeth* at Hampton Court shows a great patronage artist who worked at the same level as Lope de Vega, Calderón and Molière, and the play retains its fascination for royalty: there is a striking photograph of Prince Charles as Macbeth, taken at Gordonstoun in 1965. For Shakespeare, that command performance was his, and the King's Men's, last sighting of Hampton Court. With the exception of a couple of plays put on at Greenwich Palace (a venue which no longer exists), their stage performances at court were held always in Whitehall Palace.

First Gentleman	Sir,

You must no more call it York Place. That's past;
For since the cardinal fell, that title's lost.
'Tis now the King's, and called Whitehall.

(*Henry VIII*, 4.1.94–7)

That comes in a scene now reckoned to be Fletcher's work. It has the hallmark of Fletcher's style in this play, a trick of knowingness coming from a court insider. Act IV, scene 1 is 'the card or calendar of gentry', with the audience informed that 'York Place' is passé, and the only proper term is Whitehall. Even so, 'Whitehall' is a slightly misleading name, suggesting as it does a single building designed as a whole. The palace actually covered twenty-three acres, and an Italian visitor noted that the palace was 'nothing more than an assemblage of several houses, built at different times and for different purposes' (Kernan, *Shakespeare*, p. 52). It did not have that integrated, purposeful design that made Hampton Court, as transformed by Sir Christopher Wren in the 1690s, such a commanding symbol of state. In the Tudor era, plays at Whitehall were put on in a wooden structure, a large banqueting house which was erected to hold entertainments. As so often in England, a creation supposed to be temporary lasted long. It was burned down in 1606, and James decided to replace it with a permanent building of brick and stone, planned to be part of a vast new palace which would compare with the Escorial and the Louvre. James made a beginning with the Banqueting House, completed in 1609. It was a free-standing building that provided space for large-scale entertainments. The Great Hall and the smaller Great Chamber were also used for performances, for which temporary seating would be set up along the sides and at the back of the hall. For all performances, the seating of the king followed the cardinal rule, that he should above all be seen. As James put it in *Basilikon Doron*, 'A king is as one set on a stage, whose smallest actions and gestures, all the people gazingly do behold.' This rebuilt Banqueting House was the structure that Shakespeare would have known; but it too was destroyed by fire in 1619. The Banqueting House we see today is the work of Inigo Jones.

The Whitehall Shakespeare knew saw a brilliant season of plays for the revels of 1604–5. For this period we do have the titles, as well as the dates. When the Christmas revels began on St Stephen's Night, the opening play was *Measure for Measure* by 'Shaxberd'. This was a 'new play', therefore to be valued on that account. Later came revivals of *The Comedy of Errors*, *Love's Labour's Lost*, *Henry V* and *The*

Merchant of Venice. Remarkably, this last play was repeated two days later; James must have found its legal arguments highly congenial. Ben Jonson was also honoured for the court choice; *Every Man Out of His Humour* was played on 8 January, and *Every Man in His Humour on Candlemas* (2 February). But Shakespeare was and remained throughout his life the house dramatist of the King's Men, and the court. The rebuilt Banqueting House (1619) did indeed see the triumph of the masque, and the flawed partnership between Inigo Jones and Jonson. Shakespeare, with his acute sense of new trends, was clearly heading in the direction of the masque in *The Tempest.* That was one of the Shakespeare plays put on in Whitehall for the 1612–13 season, and was one of his last appearances at court.

That *Measure for Measure* was chosen to start the Christmas season in 1604 tells us something about the play. St Stephen's Night was the position of honour, much as the new artistic director of the Royal National Theatre has often chosen to begin his reign with *Hamlet*, and the Revels officials must have judged the play suitable for the occasion. The king may well have found *Measure for Measure* much to his taste, for Shakespeare had put on stage a ruler who has something in common with the real king but is not identical with him. The king's concerns with law and justice were treated, but not in such a way that the audience might suspect a direct contemporary reference. The issues are perennial: corrupt judges, punitive laws that are excessively enforced, human nature itself. And the king? Duke Vincentio does seem to have an echo of James himself, in

> I love the people,
> But do not like to stage me to their eyes,
> Though it do well, I do not relish well
> Their loud applause and aves vehement. (1.1.167)

But since this same belief was publicly expressed by James, coarsely, he could hardly have taken offence at Vincentio's position. Shakespeare, as always, knew what he was doing. Not for him the misjudgements of Middleton, Jonson and Marston, whose loose tongues on stage led to the severe displeasure of the authorities – and to a spell in prison.

Measure for Measure portrays the immense powers of the king's justice, and its limitations. It was fittingly presented at Whitehall.

Hampton Court and Whitehall were the two palaces which framed Shakespeare's career as a court playwright. The Whitehall he knew has passed away, though the present-day Banqueting House stands on the site of the old building. Hampton Court, transformed by Wren, still projects the glory of a royal palace, an English rejoinder to Versailles. Of all the locations that Shakespeare knew, it is the one that most fitly enshrines his status as the king's playwright.

eight
WINDSOR AND
THE MERRY WIVES

Windsor Castle.
Courtesy of the Royal Borough of Windsor & Maidenhead.

SHAKESPEARE knew his Windsor.

> *Simple:* 'There comes my master, Master Shallow, and another
> gentleman, from Frogmore, over the stile, this way.'
>
> (3.1.30–2)

There can be no more innocuous phrase than 'over the stile, this way'.
No editor would dream of giving those five words a footnote. Yet they
are at the heart of this play's imaginative concept. There must have been
members of the audience who knew exactly that very stile on the way
to Frogmore. *The Merry Wives of Windsor* is set explicitly in a town well
known to the audience, and of course to Shakespeare himself; the audience is constantly reminded of local topography and detail. This comedy
is grounded, *imagined*, in Windsor. Its hallmark is total authenticity.

And yet it does not start in Windsor. The felt location of the play, its
imaginative setting, comes to the audience in three phases. The first is the
Cotswolds. Shallow opens the play in high dudgeon against Falstaff: 'he
shall not abuse Robert Shallow, Esquire'. 'In the county of Gloucester,
Justice of Peace and coram' adds Slender helpfully. In the first five lines
we have a notable character, well remembered from *Henry IV*, Part Two,
whose position in the world is exactly matched to Shallow's regional location. In the same scene comes Slender's enquiry to Page, 'How does your
fallow greyhound, sir? I hear he was outrun on Cotswold.' (1.1.81–2). The
Cotswold Hills were famous for coursing. They are some ninety miles
from Windsor. In the next scene there's a reference to 'Banbury cheese'
(a joke, because it was noted for its thinness, like Slender). Banbury is a
road as well as a place. It is on the way to Windsor, but we have not got
there yet.

Why should we dally in the Cotswolds? Surely, because the *Merry
Wives* closely follows in time *Henry IV*, Part Two. That must have been
a success, and Shakespeare is milking a hit for its afterglow. There is
another possibility. Suppose Shakespeare himself played Shallow? It is
well within his range. We can be sure of three of Shakespeare's own parts.

He was Hamlet's Ghost, and Adam in *As You Like It*. In Ben Jonson's *Every Man in His Humour* he is listed as playing 'Kno'well, *an old gentleman*'. The pattern is suggestive: Shakespeare liked to play parts that were not especially demanding, but enabled him to make an impression and then leave the stage. Justice Shallow is in fact a highly desirable role. It was claimed by Olivier in the great Old Vic production of 1944, of whose scenes in Shallow's orchard Kenneth Tynan wrote: 'If I had only half an hour more to spend in theatres, and could choose at large, no hesitation but I would have these.' Shakespeare wrote in a *Merry Wives* part to suit himself, in which he has little to do after the opening. He then has to extricate himself from the apparent needs of his own plotting. This he does dexterously. The transition comes in 1.3, where Falstaff's opening line announces that we are at the Garter Inn. Now where is that? The clue is in the name.

The second phase gives us our fix on the play's location, when Mistress Quickly wants us to know how important she is, and where we are. 'Never a woman in Windsor knows more of Anne's mind than I do' (1.4.122–3). Mistress Page confirms the address, with her jest about the tempest that 'threw this whale ashore ... at Windsor' (2.1.600). And the sense of town comes over with Mistress Quickly's 'when the court lay at Windsor' (2.2.59–60) and her rhapsody to the Quality that is everywhere to be seen on the great court occasion. *OK!* Would be her journal of choice. She staples the point in the minds of the audience, with three more references to Windsor (2.2.95, 110, 114). We have it. The play's title means what it says.

And then the play goes on to enlarge our sense of place, making the system a kind of sat nav. The Garter Host says, 'go you through the town to Frogmore' (2.3.67–8) and 'Go about the fields with me through Frogmore' (2.3.79–80). That is very specific, and is still more so in Simple's response to the question, 'which way have you looked for Master Caius?'

'Marry, Sir, the Petty-Ward, the Park-Ward, every way; Old Windsor way, and every way but the town way' (3.1.5–7). He means the way towards Windsor Little Park, then towards Windsor Great Park. Old Windsor is a village south of Frogmore. These specifics are filled in with 'There comes my master, Master Shallow, and another gentleman, from Frogmore, over the stile, this way' (3.1.30–2). After that the local allusions come on thick and fast. The central 'pivot' scene – as so often in Shakespeare's plan of organization – is 3.3, when Mistress Ford charges the basket-carriers, John and Robert, 'be ready here hard by in the brew-house'. They are then 'to trudge with it in all haste, and carry it among the whitsters in Datchet Mead, and there empty it in the

Schloss Hohentübingen gate (above). Shakespeare refers to 'a Duke of Iarmanie' in the First Folio text. Close-up of motto engraved on the gate. (inset).
© University of Tübingen/
Friedhelm Albrecht

muddy ditch close by the Thames side' (3.3.9–14). Her house is within walking distance of the Park (3.3.211–12) and the outraged Ford is coming 'with all the officers in Windsor', and 'with half Windsor at his heels', to catch his erring wife in flagrante (3.3.101, 108). That resourceful woman, prompted by Mistress Page, knows what to do. Falstaff is bundled – with great comic possibilities – into the buck-basket, and the men are told: 'Carry them to the laundress in Datchet Mead' (139–40). Even this address becomes more precise, when Falstaff reports that the men 'were called forth by their mistress to carry me in the name of foul clothes to Datchet Lane' (3.5.91–2). 'Mead' has been sharpened to 'Lane'.

The fourth act widens the sense of neighbourhood. Brentford ('Brainsford') is a nearby village where the fat old woman dwells, much hated by Ford (4.2.66, 76). It turns out that the German confidence-ring 'has cozened all the hosts of Reading ('Readings'), of Maidenhead, of Colnbrook' (4.5.72–3). And there is Eton. Bardolph is ditched by the Germans 'so soon as I came beyond Eton' (4.4.62–3), after which the focus sharpens to the marriage of Anne Page: 'marry her at Eton' (4.4.72), with Slender 'at Eton/Immediately to marry' (4.6.24–5), whereupon 'I came yonder at Eton to marry Mistress Anne Page' (5.5.181–2). The event itself takes place in the 'Deanery' (5.3.3, 5.5.198). Eton is just across the bridge, on the other side of the Thames from Windsor.

In the third phase, the specifics of place crowd in towards the Castle. Mistress Page broaches the matter of 'Herne the Hunter, / Sometime a keeper here in Windsor Forest' (4.4.25–6), which leads to 'Herne's Oak' by which many fear to walk at night (4.4.36). In the plot to terrify Falstaff, the children are to hide and then 'Let them from forth a sawpit rush at once' (4.4.51). A sawpit was a pit across which timber was laid to be sawn, and they were a feature of Windsor Forest. Page incites his confederates, 'Come, come, we'll couch i'th'Castle ditch till we see the lights of the fairies,' a stage direction as dialogue. The same kind of direction is on Falstaff's lips at the start of 5.5, 'The Windsor bell hath struck twelve.' The entire passage is a sat nav pointing the audience towards its true destination, Windsor Castle. And to Mistress Quickly's great invocation as *Queen of Fairies*:

> About, about!
> Search Windsor Castle, elves, within and out.
> Strew good luck, ouphs, on every sacred room,
> That it may stand till the perpetual doom
> In state as wholesome as in state 'tis fit,
> Worthy the owner and the owner it.
> The several chairs of order look you scour
> With juice of balm and every precious flower.
> Each fair instalment, coat, and several crest,
> With loyal blazon, evermore be blest!
> And nightly meadow-fairies, look you sing,
> Like to the Garter's compass, in a ring.
> Th'expressure that it bears, green let it be,
> More fertile-fresh than all the field to see;
> And honi soit qui mal y pense write.
> In em'rald tufts, flowers purple, blue, and white,
> Like sapphire, pearl, and rich embroidery,
> Buckled below fair knighthood's bending knee.
> Fairies use flowers for their charactery. (5.5.55–73)

Shakespeare has made Windsor his town, with a fidelity and accuracy that is astonishing and unparalleled in the canon. The unseen words – 'hard by' occurs four times – all point in the direction that the author intends: *we are there*. And at the play's climax of location, Queen Elizabeth and Windsor Castle come together. It is a homage to Queen and Castle, monarch and realm. The audience has been conducted on a journey from Gloucestershire to Windsor, and to the centre of the town's identity: the final message is YOU HAVE REACHED YOUR DESTINATION.

nine

RICHARD III'S ENGLAND

WHEN I first saw Olivier's film of *Richard III*, it happened to be in a Tewkesbury cinema. The audience was unprepared for its starring role in certain passages, and reacted joyously to 'whom I, some three months since, / Stabbed in my angry mood at Tewkesbury'

Tower of London.
© Historic Royal Palaces. Photograph: Nick Guttridge.

(1.2.243–4) and 'false, fleeting, perjured Clarence, / That stabbed me in the field by Tewkesbury' (1.4.55–6). Taken by surprise, the locals loved it. 'To think that we're in Shakespeare! Us!' Ever since then, I've been alerted to the theatrical role of place-naming in Shakespeare. All the histories are full of such names. In *Richard III* it's a major strategy.

No play of Shakespeare's is so strongly imbued with a sense of place, of national identity as the sum of many locations. Counting indifferently together names of places and titles (I shall come to the distinction later), I find some fifty English locations mentioned, whether of house (Crosby House), county (Devonshire) or city (Exeter). Of these fifty, many are referred to on several occasions. The Tower of London is mentioned no fewer than twenty-five times. All the major regions of the country are covered. The cumulative effect is of a massive impregnation of the text with a sense of England, the full extent of the land.

For each single allusion to a place, there is a justification peculiar to drama. Some member of the audience will know it, or have some connection there. Shakespeare must have learned early that the chances of striking a chord in a spectator's mind, through the allusion to some out-of-the-way place, are fairly high. Someone always turns out to have come from Haverfordwest. It is not unlike the well-known odds against finding two people with identical birthdays in a quite small group. And the London references must connect with virtually the entire audience.

The effect of each reference is a minor shock of recognition. The place-names are tiny foci of dramatic energy, pellets of meaning released into the audience's bloodstream. 'I used to live near Barnard's Castle.' 'You *can* stay at Stony Stratford, but I wouldn't, not with the inns there.' 'Curious how you can always get good strawberries in Holborn. Richard's quite right there.' 'My mother came from Hereford!' And so on. Much dramatic energy is stored away in these innocent namings.

If that were all, it would at least justify raising the matter. But Shakespeare does not deploy place-names on a scatter principle. He organizes these far-flung places into patterns which are, as I take it, his sense of the audience's identity.

In Act I, *Richard III* is above all a London play. Set in London, the milieu has great solidity of impression. The many references to the Tower, with all its associations, symbolize the dramatic centre of London, and we hear of Chertsey, St Paul's, Crosby House (where Richard lives), Whitefriars. The provinces exist only through the references to St Albans and Tewkesbury (and thus, the past of the civil wars). Through this phase the audience enjoys the greatest rapport with Richard. Broadly, then: in the first act we are Londoners in London, and we approve of Richard.

Act II begins the move away. Although the play is still set in London, the impress of topography is much weaker. The talk is of travel, of Ludlow, Stony Stratford, Northampton. It is an undular strategy, in which Shakespeare creates a psychic wave away from London.

Act III anchors itself very firmly in London. All the manoeuvrings take place there, and the citizenry must establish itself as belonging to the capital. Similarly with the Recorder, and the Lord Mayor of London. We are reminded of Holborn, the Crown, Baynard's Castle, Tower Bridge, St Paul's, Crosby House. The provinces (Pomfret (=Pontefract), Hereford) are still at the margins of this play's consciousness. At the height of its pleasure at Richard's performance, the audience is continually reminded: this is London, our city.

The peremptory 'Stand all apart' (4.2.1) announces the second half of the play. That order to the courtiers figures Richard's relations with the audience. From now on he is distrustful, paranoid. The old rapport is gone. The allusions to place impart the new reality. We have no sense of London, though the play is still set there. All the talk is of the provinces, which now come to the fore of the play's consciousness. The roll-call is impressive: Exeter, Brecknock, Salisbury, Devonshire, Kent, Yorkshire, Dorsetshire, Milford, Pembroke, Haverfordwest. The west, Wales, even Kent are up in arms. The north (of the 'cold friends') is the distrusted, hostage-enforced alliance with Derby. The drama, then, composes a map which we can discern without much difficulty: the great rough triangle of the British Isle has arrows pointed, threateningly, towards London. And with them the psychology of the play changes. The provinces are right, and London is wrong.

With these explicit indications come subliminal suggestions that tend to the same end. Place-names go beyond the simple symbolism of region and rebellion. There's a soft mutation of *place* to *title*. The play often broods on 'title', as Brakenbury does – Richard, the Duchess of

York, Queen Elizabeth all talk about it – and the union of place and name has great significance. We have largely lost our sense of it today, with our later traditions of title based on surname or battle honour or simple euphony allied to tenuous local connection (Attlee, Alamein, Avon). It is salutary to be reminded, as one can still be in England today, that a local magnate counts for something in the area bearing his name. Titles were based on the possession of land; they were not empty honorifics. A name signified a reality. Thus insidiously the play makes its point: Dorset (the Marquess of Dorset) may be a cipher, but Dorsetshire (4.4.522) matters. The titles, hence the land, are up in arms against the king.

And who supports the king? The symbolism of Act V is clear. Only from the south-east is there any support: the Duke of Norfolk and the Earl of Surrey, his son. (The name of Richard's horse, 'White Surrey', underlines the symbolism.) Outside the south-east only Northumberland sides with Richard, and he is dubious, stigmatized as 'melancholy'and having his conversation repeated for Richard's benefit ('What said Northumberland as touching Richmond?'). Derby has already made his arrangements. The titles offer a diagram of forces here.

The conclusion is a boar-hunt, conducted in the middle of England:

> Thus far into the bowels of the land
> Have we marched on without impediment …
> The wretched, bloody, and usurping boar,
> That spoiled your summer fields and fruitful vines,
> Swills your warm blood like wash, and makes his trough
> In your embowelled bosoms, this foul swine
> Is now even in the centre of this isle,
> Near to the town of Leicester, as we learn. (5.2.3–4, 7–12)

We have lately learned that Richard remains in the town of Leicester, re-interred in Leicester Cathedral. It is indeed close to Bosworth, almost 'the centre of the isle'. There the forces of the south and west, united with the Midlands (Oxford), defeat the tyrant, who is let down by the north and inadequately defended by his own south-east. The land renews itself, gathering together to kill the usurper to its title. Again, as in *King John*,

Shakespeare plays on the synecdoche of 'England' and 'King of England'. The triumph of right is also the triumph of the provinces. The alienation of the London audience is now complete: it detaches itself from 'the bloody dog' and declares itself for the morality of the provinces, and thus the nation. Title (the Crown), land, people and audience unite. The many place-names are the underplot of the land bonding against the tyrant; in the end, the bonding principle of the audience is that it is English. Without an atlas, the Histories cannot be understood; location really is everything. 'Geography is about maps,' said E. C. Bentley, 'but Biography is about chaps.' With Shakespeare, the chaps are named after the maps. And the maps carry as big a raft of psychology as Freud's.

ten

FALSTAFF'S TAVERN

MAN in a landscape, that is the great theme of art from the Renaissance on. The subject of the painting dwells in a landscape or background which illustrates and extends him. It is his world. To get at Falstaff, we have to understand his world, or rather the scene in which he characteristically appears. It is the tavern.

Stone tavern sign of the Boar's Head, London, 1668.
© Museum of London.

We know more about tavern life than any other area of English life in the first part of *Henry IV.* The textures of ordinary life are imparted with extraordinary density in the two great scenes, 2.4 and 3.3. As David Bevington puts it,

> The sense of locale for a tavern is created in the *Henry IV* plays not only by tables, stools, tapsters in their leather aprons, whores with their ruffs and jewels, 'lack-linen' swaggerers with swords and 'two points' on their shoulder, musicians, drinking companies with red countenances, talk of 'mouldy stewed prunes and dried cakes', quantities of sack and the like, but by a sense of enclosed space defined by two unseen presences, one of the interior rooms of the tavern and the other the outside world. (*Action is Eloquence* (Harvard University Press, 1944), p. 132)

This 'interior room' is what we know most about. To this vital space is added the inn yard just outside. In the Rochester inn yard scene (2.1) we learn of fleas, damp provender, staffing problems since the departure of the lamented Robin Ostler, the insanitary habits of the English, and the breakfast order of the travellers who 'call for eggs and butter'. The tavern, with its interior and its inn yard, is the focus of life as it is lived.

One could write an extended and no doubt largely accurate description of Elizabethan day-to-day realities, simply on the basis of the tavern scenes. It is symbolically apt that Hal, at the beginning of the great tavern scene, presents himself in the role of observer come to study the linguistic and cultural ways of the English at their pleasures. 'I can drink with any tinker in his own language during my life' (2.4.18–19). He seems a cultural anthropologist, come from abroad to study the habitat and mores of this strange tribe, the English. He does it, and we could do it; the information is all there.

Note that we could accomplish nothing remotely comparable on the basis of the court/rebel scenes. Their interest is human and political, but they are not embedded in the minutiae of everyday life. Technically, they are not so much thin as light, their context touched in with a few pencil strokes. It is the same principle as in *Twelfth Night*, where we could say a great deal about Olivia's household and very little about Orsino's court.

The one locale stands out with stereoscopic intensity, the other is recessed and devoid of telling detail. Thus, the scenes in Part One which engage our emotions most profoundly are those rooted in the real, in which there are many physical enhancements of the experience.

Next, the tavern scenes are a defined type of room scene. 'The room', says J. E. Cirlot, in *A Dictionary of Symbols* (Philosophical Press, 1962), 'is a symbol of individuality, of private thoughts.' That may not seem to describe closely the tavern, with its multiple membership and sense of communal life. Nevertheless, the tavern is given over to the free play of individuality. The tavern is the home of *homo ludens*, man at ease with himself and his fellows. 'Shall I not take mine ease in mine inn?' asks Falstaff (*1 Henry IV*, 3.3.81). In this parenthesis of being, man is free to discover himself. The room is also, as we saw in 2.4, an auditorium. Prince Hal is a young man in search of identity and self. ('I shall hereafter, my thrice gracious liege, / Be more myself' (3.2.92–3). Those words are the dead centre of the pivot scene.) That self is the image of his kingly father: duty and authority.

And where did he learn of that self? In the Boar's Head, where the freedom of the mimic games enabled him to change places with Falstaff. 'Dost thou speak like a king? Do thou stand for me, and I'll play my father' (2.4.428–9). The self is a public one, triumphantly vindicated in Westminster and on the fields of Shrewsbury and Agincourt. But that self is first rehearsed in a private room in a tavern.

The tavern is also a refuge against the outside world. A. E. Housman set his tavern against the tempest outside: 'The doors clap to, the pane is blind with showers. / Pass me the can, lad; there's an end to May.' Shakespeare's tavern is an enclosed world where there is vast freedom to express oneself, but which is constantly under threat from without. It is, I think, a principle that all messages from outside seem threatening, if not actually so. Harold Pinter's *The Room* is the modern archetype. They disturb at least the mood, if not the well-being of the actors. We can see this principle illustrated in what is essentially a tavern scene in *Twelfth Night*, 2.3. The carousals of Sir Toby, Sir Andrew and Feste are first interrupted by Maria's warning, then closed down by the arrival of Malvolio. It is so with the tavern scene in *1 Henry IV*, 2.4. The Hostess comes to Hal with the news that 'there is a nobleman of the court at door who would speak with you: he says he comes from your father' (2.4.284–6). That is a call that the Prince chooses to ignore, or rather declassify: the message from father is converted to ridicule via Falstaff. 'Do thou stand for my father and examine me upon the particulars of my life' (372–3). At the end of the play episode comes '*A knocking heard. Exeunt Hostess, Francis, and Bardolph. Enter Bardolph, running*': 'O my lord, my lord, the sheriff with a most monstrous watch is at your door' (477–8). A few moments of agitated exchange pass, Falstaff and others make themselves scarce, then '*Enter Sheriff and the Carrier.*' The party is over.

My point is that the mood is defined by the threat. Without this cold penetration from the outside world we would not understand so well the quality of being created inside the tavern. The Prince does, after all, have to handle a police inquiry, one which concerns a genuine crime. The outside world insists on its right to redefine what, to the taverners, is a glorious and profitable prank. The later stages of this scene might well be subtitled 'An Inspector Calls'. This outside world is that of the court, the political and military establishment, society itself. It is difficult, complex, often threatening, and real. Moreover, it seeks to reclassify tavern life as base, untrustworthy and aberrant. Taverners take refuge from that world. Hence the archetypal gesture of the taverners is Falstaff's 'Hostess, clap to the doors' (2.4.273), and the archetypal threat is *knocking*. Is there a more disturbing sound, anywhere, than *knocking*?

In the presence of Falstaff we experience a 'release into sudden freedom'. Mark Rose's phrase, in *Shakespearean Design* (Harvard University Press, 1972), points to its pole, discipline and restraint. M. M. Mahood, in *Shakespeare's Wordplay* (Methuen, 1957), catches the implications: 'Falstaff, whose very charm lies in the way he represents freedom from all normal inhibitions, even succeeds in breaking down those of the Lord Chief Justice, that walking embodiment of Freud's Censor, to the point where he too begins to pun.' That refers to the Chief Justice's final line to Falstaff, 'You are too impatient to bear crosses' ('crosses' = afflictions, coins, *2 Henry IV*, 1.2.213). The contest between the Life Force and the Censor has a first innings, Part One, in which the Life Force takes a clear lead. The second innings, Part Two, is a clear victory for the Censor. The Lord Chief Justice appears only in Part Two. It is his emissary, the Sheriff, who appears in Part One to disturb the revels. The series of interruptions to the life of the tavern, from Sir John Bracy (the King's Messenger, intercepted by Falstaff) to the Sheriff and Carrier, who are met but are not to be put off, points towards the origin of the threats: King and Father, the Censor and the Law. From these forces the taverners take refuge.

The tavern scene of 3.3 in *2 Henry IV* makes the same points more brusquely. The by-play with Hostess, Falstaff and the Prince is now a mere interlude. Hal has news: 'I have procured thee, Jack, a charge of foot' (186). And Hal's talk is all of business: 'Go, Peto, to horse, to horse, for thou and I / Have thirty miles to ride yet ere dinner time' (187–8). The tavern has now changed its psychic map reference. From being fixed in Eastcheap, it is now a post-house on the road to Coventry. It is left to Falstaff to sound the note of regret and loss at this transformation: 'O, I could wish this tavern were my drum!' (206).

The tavern is the setting for Falstaff and the most characteristic and inward scenes of Part One. It is the container for the pleasure principle. And all the time there plays upon the life of the tavern that draught from the outside world, the chill wind of war, business, affairs of state, a redefinition of experience. Beyond the tavern lies – to simplify the reference – the court. The court means something very different from what we habitually understand. It is not a graceful appendage to the real world, designer history, but the thing itself, the centre of power and state action. When Hal says, 'I'll to the Court in the morning' (*1 Henry IV*, 2.4.517) he means that he's going to work. Hal knows what Feste knows: 'Truly, sir, and pleasure will be paid, one time or another' (*Twelfth Night*, 2.4.70–1). In this escape from Time and its cares, the tavern is best seen as a version of pastoral.

eleven

JONSON'S LONDON

IF anyone invented the author, it was Ben Jonson. His remorseless self-promotion marked him out as the first literary celebrity. When he went on his famous walk to Scotland in 1618 (with a companion, surely a bag-carrier) he was met everywhere by local dignitaries and emissaries of great houses, beseeching Jonson to stay with them. Outside Berwick-upon-Tweed, church bells were rung and volleys of shot fired in Jonson's honour, as Ian Donaldson tells us in his definitive biography (*Ben Jonson: A Life*, Oxford University Press, 2011). A crowd welcomed him at Mercat Cross, Edinburgh. This was fame.

Detail from Claes Visscher's panorama of London, 1616.
© Museum of London.

How did he do it? First, by asserting his public claim as owner of his plays. This was new. The first half-dozen of Shakespeare's plays to be published as quartos bear no sign of authorship; not till 1598 did *Love's Labour's Lost* come out as Shakespeare's, and by then he was famous. Jonson's early efforts have not survived, but *Every Man in His Humour* (1598) was a hit, and the quarto ('The Author B.I.') appeared in 1601. After that there was no holding him. Jonson's addresses to the public, like George Bernard Shaw's prefaces, make *the author* a living and vital presence. Before *Volpone*, for example, he tells us

> 'Tis known, five weeks fully penned it,
> From his own hand, without a coadjutor,
> Novice, journeyman, or tutor.

Unlike Shakespeare, who prefers to disappear behind his plays, Jonson constantly points to himself as their creator and origin.

Then, Jonson understood that a major literary figure must situate himself in London. In *The Alchemist* (1610) comes

> Our scene is London, 'cause we would make known,
> No country's mirth is better than our own:

Jonson's Prologue to *The Alchemist* drives a stake into the ground, claiming the territory for his own. He had previously had fun with *Volpone* (1606):

> Most noble gentlemen, and my worthy patrons, it may seem strange
> that I, your Scoto Mantuano, who was ever wont to fix my bank in face
> ot the public Piazza, near the shelter of the Portico to the Procuratia,
> should now, after eight months' absence from the illustrious city of
> Venice, humbly retire myself into an obscure nook of the Piazza.

But thereafter exotic locations were set aside, and Jonson settled on London for his comic art. A metropolitan writer needs the metropolis. More, the never-ending growth of the city, both in population and importance, drove up the role of the stage – and its pre-eminent writer. In this rapidly changing scene, playing companies became London-based, moving away from their touring past. All this gave Jonson his opportunity: he consistently asserted authorial identity by emphasizing drama's power to represent space. And, of course, the author. Jonson did not disappear into his works.

One can overdo the argument that Shakespeare and Jonson are clean different as authors. The excellent proof-reading, and self-identification of *Venus and Adonis* and *The Rape of Lucrece* show that Shakespeare was not unaware of the advantages of a successful poet with a decent text. The two poems were the acceptable face of soft porn. Still, Jonson's incessant self-promotion, and care over editing his texts, was something new in literary history. He brought out his *Workes* (1616) in his lifetime, when he had two decades to go, while Shakespeare's Folio (1623), edited by his colleagues, appeared posthumously. In Jonson's *Workes* the plays are presented chronologically, so that they give a history of Jonson's development.

Jonson helped to invent the new genre of 'city comedy', but that is not a fully adequate term. He shapes the meaning of London as stage for his interpretive art, and here his chronology becomes significant. Florence had been the nominal setting for *Every Man in His Humour* in the quarto version (1601), a thinly disguised account of the English metropolis with its fashions and trends. The revised text published in *Workes* takes London explicitly as the envelope for the action. Here the sense of social immediacy is intensified, and the play's setting is shifted to easily recognizable neighbourhoods of London. The places named have powerful metaphorical significance: Bordello, Pict-Hatch (the prostitution district of Clerkenwell), Mile End (where the amateur city militia trained). Topography is character and 'humour', and takes on a deeper meaning. The quarto had the meeting place as 'Friary', but the assignation spot was transformed in the *Workes* to the Tower of London. The Tower was both a prison and a 'liberty', an area outside city jurisdiction. Wellbred and Edward Kno'well redefined it by their flight as a symbol of individual freedom. Even so, the Tower of London remained what it was in *Richard III*, a menacing icon of state power. Jonson's London offers a model of space and place applicable to the everyday, 'real' urban experience. The playwright sees dramatic authorship primarily as a way of representing and rewriting the city.

London is a city of places, to be rendered into a stage. One performance is *On The Famous Voyage* (1610), Jonson's gleefully scatological journey along the Thames. He transforms Fleet Ditch into Hades, a celebration of his interpretive art. Jonson is not the first or last to note that a great river disposes of a city's sewage, but he makes it into an epic journey. The *Voyage* complements a higher order of treatment in the 1604 Royal Entrance of James I. In *Part of King James His Entertainment*, Jonson makes the claim that the reader has a more complete and perfect experience of the royal entry than any experience available on the actual day. The Genius of London is anatomized, with much detail on the Fenchurch Street arch. Jonson equates urban space with page space, and he designed the final device of the pageant to be performed in the Strand. Urban space is a medium through which to present his authority.

The *Workes* texts of *Epicoene* and *The Alchemist* specify 'THE SCENE LONDON'. Lovewit's 'house in town', staged at the Blackfriars, offers an equivalence between stage and playhouse. There is an exact parallel between the activities of the con artists and Jonson's theatrics, creating in *The Alchemist* a sense of ironic complicity between the players and the rogues they depict. This is a consciously metatheatrical comedy. In this fixed, plague-emptied space entrances and exits are the play itself, with the door the central locus. The conmen are *players*: 'Do we not / Sustain our parts?' And the audience may discover a version of themselves. In the final epilogue-like speeches of Lovewit and Face the voice of the character merges with the player.

Bartholomew Fair (1614) looks to be the last of Jonson's great London plays, the summation of everything he had worked towards. The action is in Smithfield, which has its own character, its own 'humour'; 'Thou art the seat of the beast, o Smithfield, and I will leave thee. Idolatry peepeth out on every side of thee,' says the fanatical Puritan Zeal-of-the-land Busy. Even today, Londoners often refer to their city as a collection of villages, and Jonson would assent. Particular local spots are mentioned thirty times, and *place* occurs forty-seven times. The unities of place and time mean that the play takes place on 24 August, St Bartholomew's Day. And yet the play is not included in the *Workes*. This is an unsolved puzzle, and we can only guess at Jonson's reasons. We can take *Bartholomew Fair* as a forerunner to greater work by Bunyan and Thackeray: *Vanity Fair*. Jonson's London is the fullest realization of the dramatic poet, in every sense, and it still is. He was buried in Westminster Abbey, vertically and upside down. For Jonson it was 'My way', from first to last.

<h1 style="text-align:center">twelve</h1>

<h1 style="text-align:center">BEN JONSON AT
ALTHORP</h1>

<h3 style="text-align:center">Memoir of a Royal Visit</h3>

A*LTHORP, Althrop.* The ancestral seat of Earl Spencer has been much in view since it now memorializes Diana, Princess of Wales. But the name puzzled commentators. During broadcast commentaries, speakers took care to pronounce it 'Althrop.' Herford and Simpson, in the second volume of their edition of Jonson (1923), note of 'Althrope' that 'this pronunciation is still locally current'.[1] By the time they arrived

Althorp.
© David Humphreys/Alamy.

at volume ten (1950), they stated that 'Althrop' was the old pronunciation of Althorp, 'but it is rare now: the fifth Earl Spencer always used
it'.[2] The present Earl Spencer has now laid it down that the correct pronunciation is as spelt, 'Althorp'. The guides on the estate loyally follow
this edict.

Jonson's stay at Althorp led to *A Particular Entertainment of the
Queen and Prince their Highnesse to Althrope, at the Right Honourable
the Lord Spencers, on Saterday being the 25. of June 1603 as they came first
unto the Kingdome; being written by the same Author, and not before published*. That was the 1604 quarto. In 1616 Jonson brought out his *Workes*,
in folio, in which the place is again 'Althrope'. The *Entertainment*,
an early essay in the masque genre, commemorates a notable occasion.
The old Queen, Elizabeth I, had died in March 1603. Her successor was
James, the sixth of Scotland, the first of England, who in the summer
made his way from Edinburgh to London. En route he accepted many
offers of hospitality at the great houses, the owners desperate to secure
the favour of the new king. One such was Sir Robert Spencer, who,
says the *Dictionary of National Biography*, 'at the accession of James
I was reputed the wealthiest man in England'. Much of Spencer's
money came from sheep-breeding, to which he had devoted himself.
He wished to secure his status under the new regime, and pulled off his
coup: the Queen and Prince stopped off for four days at the Spencer
family seat.

Something more than standard hospitality was required. An entertainment had to be laid on. Sir Robert went to the best man in town,
Ben Jonson. Jonson was not yet famous for his masques, those opulent
and expensive court entertainments, but his poetic and dramatic gifts
were well established. Like Sir Robert, he wanted an *entrée* to the new
court. He accepted the commission to devise an entertainment, which
entailed travelling to Althorp and to be on standby for the great event.
Jonson thus became Writer in Residence at Althorp. The salient facts
of the entertainment were these: it was to be presented before Queen
Anne – a great lover of the theatre – and her young son, Prince Henry.
And the setting was one of the patches of woodland close to the great
house, in what is rolling parkland. Jonson explains his thinking in the
stage direction, which opens the entertainment:

The invention was, to have a Satyre lodged in a little Spinet [spinney or copse], *by which her Maiestie, and the Prince were to come, who (at the report of certayne Cornets that were divided in severall places of the Parke, to signify her approach) advanced his head above the top of the wood, wondring, and (with his pipe in his hand) began as follows.*[3]

The royal party would have been comfortably seated in the 'spinet'. We know from the Household Accounts of Althorp that good care was taken.[4] The items include

Itm to iij woomen weeding ij dayes
a peece in the new spynneye
and in the double hedge in the wyndmill field

More was paid out to women 'setting up ivy' in the garden. Eight tailors were employed sewing up canvas (presumably, for the canopy, or marquee). Sir Robert spared no expense in creating the most favourable impression for his royal guests. After the initial 'invention', the next major stage direction is

Here he ranne into the wood againe, and hid himselfe, whilst to the sound of excellent soft Musique, that was there concealed in the thicket; there came tripping up the lawne, a bevy of Faeries, attending on MAB their Queene, who falling into an artificiall ring, that was cut into the path, began to dance a round, whilst their Mistris spake as followeth.

The elegant foolery with Mab, her fairies and a lurking satyr is a courtly bringing together of diverse elements. Shakespeare had pioneered the way. 'The mischievous elves, fairies, and puckish satyr who pay homage to Queen Anne in *The Entertainment at Althorp* are reminiscent of *A Midsummer Night's Dream*.'[5]

But the key to everything is Jonson's stage directions. Stage directions are customarily given in the present tense. Here, as throughout the text of the *Entertainment* that Jonson published, the past historic

tense is that of reportage. Jonson is saying, in his own way, 'I was there.'
His stage direction now conveys with special authority an astounding
coup de théâtre:

> *At that, the whole wood and place resounded with the noyse of cornets,*
> *hornes, and other hunting musique, and a brace of choise Deere put out,*
> *and as fortunately kill'd, as they were meant to be; even in the sight of*
> *her Maiestie.*

A real killing of the deer was staged before the royal party. In
the seventeenth century, hunting often involved the enclosing of ani-
mals within the pales of a park and then slaughtering them at leisure.
This 'happening' must have been meticulously planned. 'Fortunately
kill'd' means 'In a fortunate manner', 'happily', 'successfully'. When
Jonson writes 'as they were meant to be', he means that it was no lucky
accident. There is here the iron pride, not only of the writer, but of the
impresario.

This sylvan extravaganza was on a Saturday, and on Sunday, says
Jonson, the Queen rested, as also on Monday, until after dinner,

> Where there was a speech sodainly thought on, to induce a morrise
> of the clownes thereabout, who most officiously presented them-
> selves, but by reason of the throng of the country that came in, their
> speaker could not be heard.

The 'clowns' turned up to offer their contribution – 'officiously' is a word
of praise, 'dutifully'. Jonson, as writer in residence, had to compose a
speech, 'sodainly thought on'. Naturally, he was up to it.

But a crowd of pushy locals got into the act, and prevented the
speech from being heard. The speaker *'was in the person of Nobody –*
attyred in a paire of breeches which were made to come up to his neck, with
his armes out at his pockets, and a cap drowning his face'. This uncouth rural
figure is at the origins of the antimasque, a grotesque interlude between
the acts of a masque. We can see resemblances in the pastoral scene of
The Winter's Tale, where Shakespeare's stage direction is *'Heere a Dance*
of twelve Satyres' (4.4.370). These rustic figures are 'men of hair' (hairy

men) or satyrs, Greek woodland deities translated into English vernacular. Shakespeare and Jonson are cueing into the same tradition. Jonson is by now a commentator as much as a scriptwriter, and the next stage direction is a condensed memoir:

> *There was also another parting Speech, which was to have been presented in the person of a youth, and accompanied with divers gentlemans younger sons of the countrey: but by reason of the multitudinous presse, was also hindred. And which we have here adioyned.*

Game to the last, Jonson publishes the full text of the writer-in-residence's contribution, even though it had to be cut in performance. 'Presse' is 'crowd,' of course, but there is a prophetic ring to the 'multitudinous presse' which became such a threat to good order at Althorp.

Still, the whole affair went off very well, even if a Jonsonian speech or two were tragically aborted by the unruly crowd. A jewel was presented by Queen Mab to Queen Anne, on behalf of Sir Robert Spencer, a most tactful form of words by Jonson preventing the offering from seeming too gross a bid for favour. The entertainment itself was sometimes known as *The Masque of Oriana*, since it celebrates Anne in her progress as Oriana – *quasi oriens Anna*, says its author in a note. And in another strangely resonant touch, the closing song ends

> *Long live ORIANA*
> *To excel (whom she succeeds) our late DIANA.*

And the outcome of the Althorp event was benign for all. The royal visitors must have been well content with the efforts made on their behalf. Jonson got the court patronage he craved. 'Indeed, Queen Anne's witnessing of this work may later have led her to commission Jonson's first masques for the court.'[6] Sir Robert Spencer got his peerage, and swiftly: on 21 July 1603 he was created Baron Spencer of Wormleighton. Before the year was out he was on a diplomatic mission to Wurtemberg. He had, it is true, to put up with some flouts in the House of Lords, where Arundel reminded him of the time when the Spencers were best known for keeping sheep. But it was a notable career. 'The *Entertainment* as a whole was part of Robert Spencer's bid to secure his status under the new regime; indeed, he and Jonson were in that respect similarly placed.'[7]

The consequences of that notable entertainment remain with us. The Spencer connection with the royal family continues into the House of Windsor. Prince William and Prince Harry are direct descendants of the first Baron Spencer. And the second Baron Spencer married a daughter of Henry Wriothesley, Earl of Southampton and the dedicatee of *Venus and Adonis* and *The Rape of Lucrece*. The royal house therefore claims direct descent from the great patrons of Shakespeare and Jonson, the Earl of Southampton and Baron Spencer.

Notes

1.   Ben Jonson, *Works*, ed. C. H. Herford and Percy and Evelyn Simpson, 11 vols (Clarendon Press, 1925–32), vol. II, p. 260.

2.   Jonson, *Works*, vol. X, p. 394.

3.   Stage directions are as in the text given in Jonson, *Works*, vol. VII.

4.   Details of the Household accounts are as given in Jonson, *Works*, vol. X, p. 394. Earl Spencer has published an account of the later development of Althorp: see Charles Spencer, *Althorp: The Story of a House* (Viking, 1998).

5.   W. David Kay, *Ben Jonson: A Literary Life* (Macmillan, 1995), pp. 65–6.

6.   Robert C. Evans, *Ben Jonson and the Poetics of Patronage* (Bucknell University Press, 1989), p. 227.

7.   Evans, *Ben Jonson and the Poetics of Patronage*, p. 237.

INDEX